Wasted

Kate Tempest was born in London in 1985. Her work includes the plays *Wasted, Glasshouse* and *Hopelessly Devoted*; the poetry collections *Everything Speaks in its Own Way* and *Hold Your Own*; the albums *Everybody Down, Balance, Let Them Eat Chaos* and *The Book of Traps and Lessons*; the long poems *Brand New Ancients* and *Let Them Eat Chaos*; and her debut novel, *The Bricks that Built the Houses*.

Katie Beswick is a lecturer in drama at the University of Exeter, UK. She has published widely on theatre and council estates in journals including *Research in Drama Education, Performance Research* and *New Theatre Quarterly*, and her monograph *Social Housing in Performance* was published by Methuen Drama in 2019.

Wasted

KATE TEMPEST

With commentary and notes by

KATIE BESWICK

Series Editors: Sara Freeman, Jenny Stevens, Matthew Nichols
and Chris Megson

methuen | drama

LONDON • NEW YORK • OXFORD • NEW DELHI • SYDNEY

METHUEN DRAMA

Bloomsbury Publishing Plc

50 Bedford Square, London, WC1B 3DP, UK

1385 Broadway, New York, NY 10018, USA

BLOOMSBURY, METHUEN DRAMA and the Methuen Drama logo
are trademarks of Bloomsbury Publishing Plc

Wasted first published in Great Britain 2013

This edition first published 2020

Cover design: Charlotte Daniels

Cover image: Aftermath of party in kitchen (© Andreas Grabow / Getty Images)

A catalogue record for this book is available from the British Library.

A catalog record for this book is available from the Library of Congress.

ISBN: PB: 978-1-3500-9492-5
      ePDF: 978-1-3500-9494-9
      eBook: 978-1-3500-9493-2

Series: Student Editions

Typeset by Integra Software Services Pvt. Ltd.

Printed and bound in India

To find out more about our authors and books visit www.bloomsbury.com
and sign up for our newsletters.

Contents

Chronology and Significant Historical Events

The timeline below maps an account of national and world events that surround the first performance of *Wasted*. As we will see in the CONTEXT section of this introduction, these seemingly unrelated events converge in the play in a variety of ways.

1973   11 August: Hip hop culture officially begins when teenager Clive Campbell performs as 'DJ Kool Herc' at a back-to-school party, thrown by his sister Cindy, in the recreation rooms at 1520 Sedgwick Avenue, an apartment complex in the Bronx, New York. Using two turntables to play the same record, he innovates with a technique he has perfected over the preceding months, creating extended instrumental breaks so that partygoers can dance for longer. According to hip hop legend, his friend, Coke La Rock, hypes up the crowd by rhyming over instrumentals. Three of the four 'pillars' or 'elements' of hip hop culture: DJing, MCing (rhyming over music) and break-dancing (dancing in the instrumental breaks of song) are in action that evening. The fourth pillar of hip hop, graffiti, emerges around the same period. During the 1970s, graffiti, often in the form of 'tags' (marks indicating the creator), is seen across public spaces in inner city New York. Often it covers the interior and exterior of subway cars that travel all over the city. In *New York: A Documentary Film*, cultural critic Marshall Berman describes how the subway trains provided a means through which those (black, Hispanic and working-class people) from the impoverished neighbourhood of the Bronx were able to communicate with those in more affluent areas. As he argues, graffiti was 'the earliest form in which most people who weren't part of that neighbourhood' came to understand what was happening there. Scholars who write about hip hop often argue that there are not four, but five elements; depending on who you consult, 'knowledge' is often considered the fifth element.

1979   4 May: Margaret Thatcher becomes Prime Minister of the United Kingdom, having served as Leader of the Opposition since 1975. Her leadership is characterized by fiscal conservatism, economic reliance on the free-market, privatization of state-owned industry, hostility towards trade unions and scaling back the welfare state. So-called 'Thatcherite' politics, following the model of 'Reaganomics' introduced by US President Ronald Reagan, with whom Thatcher was closely allied, marks the UK's move towards neoliberalism as an economic model (see the THEMES section for a discussion and explanation of the term 'neoliberalism').

December: The hip hop record 'Rapper's Delight' by New Jersey's the Sugarhill Gang reaches number three in the UK singles chart, marking the first mainstream success for hip hop in the United Kingdom.

1982   December: The first British hip hop record, 'Christmas Rapping' by the artist Dizzy Heights, released by Polydor Records, reaches number forty-nine in the UK singles chart, following a surge of underground and self-released hip hop music. Popular British artists, including Adam and the Ants, The Clash, Malcolm McLaren and Wham! also experiment with adopting hip hop techniques into their music throughout the early 1980s, demonstrating how hip hop is beginning to take root as part of popular culture in the UK.

1984   March: The Miners' Strike, a major industrial action staged by the National Union of Mineworkers in response to the government's attempts to close British collieries, shuts down the UK's coal industry. Thatcher attempts to quash the power of trade unions by opposing the strike. In June 1984, there is a violent clash between striking miners and the police at a coking plant in Rotherham, South Yorkshire. Known as the 'Battle of Orgreave', the event sees thousands of police officers deployed, including mounted officers and police dogs, in an attempt to overwhelm the pickets. The strike is ruled illegal in September.

1985   3 March: The Miners' Strike officially ends. This marks a significant turning point in the culture and trajectory of the British working classes. The power of trade unions is severely weakened, and in the coming decades there is rapid deindustrialization. Opportunities for working-class people to find well-paid, secure jobs with clearly defined benefits and prospects for promotion decrease, and there is an increase in unemployment, drug abuse and social instability in former working-class strongholds. The sense of community and collectivity that characterized the mid-twentieth-century working-class experience begins to fracture, as those able to participate in the neoliberal culture leave behind those who cannot. In a now famous speech delivered in 1987, Thatcher proudly champions the era of the individual, claiming that there is 'no such thing as society'.

22 December: Kate Esther Calvert is born in London. She adopts the stage and pen name Kate Tempest in the mid-2000s after performing for a number of years under the name Excentral Tempest. She is part of the so-called 'millennial' generation, a term used to describe those born between the early 1980s and the late 1990s who became adults in the new millennium. Despite a growth in progressive social movements resulting in increased rights for women, ethnic minorities and LGBT people, this group will face more financial instability than previous generations

and decreased social mobility – meaning that they are less likely than their parents to move into a higher social class or income bracket than the one they were born into.

Tempest is raised in Lewisham, in the south-east of London. The language, culture and geography of south-east London runs through her work across music, plays, novels and poetry.

1988   The British hip hop crew London Posse release 'Money Mad', a seminal track that is often considered to mark the birth of uniquely British hip hop culture. The artists use their own London accents and do not affect American-style voices as British rappers up to this point have often done. The crew also draw on dub reggae (an electronic development of reggae music), giving their music a distinctive sound that will come to distinguish British hip hop (and later the grime music that emerges from British hip hop, garage and jungle music influences) from US rap music.

1990   November: Margaret Thatcher resigns and John Major wins the leadership contest for the Conservative Party, succeeding her as Prime Minister. He goes on to win a general election in 1992.

1997   May: Labour, branded as New Labour, wins the general election and Tony Blair becomes Prime Minister. 'New Labour' is a rebranding of the Labour Party that signals a move away from its socialist roots. Blair's leadership is marked by an embrace of the free-market neoliberal ideology that has now characterized British politics since Thatcher, although he makes some concessions to reinvigorating the welfare state, notably with investment in education and Child Benefit. He vows to eliminate class inequality through an expansion of the middle classes, and pursues a social inclusion agenda based on the idea of 'equal opportunity' for all members of society. Part of this vision includes an emphasis on urban regeneration as a response to economic disadvantage. Nonetheless, despite a period of optimism based on Blairite social-democratic policies, Britain's historic class divisions remain entrenched.

2001   11 September: A series of terrorist attacks on the US using hijacked planes, most iconically bringing down the Twin Towers of the World Trade Center in New York, marks a seismic shift in global politics and the trajectory of both the UK and the US for the new millennium. George W. Bush, President of the United States, declares a 'war on terror' and the UK government, led by Blair, supports this initiative. The US and UK work in alliance to invade Afghanistan, where those held responsible for the attack were located.

2003   19 March: The US and UK launch an attack on Iraq, claiming that Iraq's leader, Saddam Hussein, is stockpiling weapons of mass destruction. The invasion goes ahead despite huge public resistance in the UK, including an anti-war march with the participation of an estimated one million citizens in London. When it is later discovered that Hussein's regime did not have the capacity to stockpile weapons of mass destruction, there is huge and growing public mistrust in the government.

2005   6 July: It is announced that London has won the bid to host the 2012 Olympics. This is a moment of huge celebration for the city. The opportunity amplifies Blair's vision for urban regeneration, and gives investors added incentive to put money towards urban development projects, particularly in run-down neighbourhoods in east and south-east London, where the Olympics will be held.

7 July: There is a series of four coordinated terrorist attacks on London, carried out by Islamic fundamentalist suicide bombers who live and were raised in the UK. They leave behind videos claiming that the attack avenges atrocities carried out by the UK as part of the War on Terror. They detonate bombs on three tube trains and a bus, killing fifty-two people.

2007   June: Gordon Brown, former Chancellor of the Exchequer, succeeds Tony Blair as Prime Minister.

2008   15 September: Following a crisis in the sub-prime mortgage market, the bank Lehman Brothers collapses, signalling an economic crisis and a massive global recession, considered by many economists to be the worst since the Great Depression in the 1930s.

2010   May: Following a general election, there is a hung parliament, meaning no single party wins an overall majority. The Conservative Party, led by David Cameron, win the most seats and form a coalition with the Liberal Democrats, ending thirteen years of Labour rule. The Cameron government introduce an 'austerity' programme, which seeks to reduce the UK's deficit by curbing public spending and tax rises. During austerity, conditions for the poorest members of British society worsen: there is an increase in the use of food banks, which provide free essentials such as food and toiletries to those in extreme poverty, and in exploitative employment practices such as zero-hours contracts, where staff are counted as 'employed' but have no guarantee of work or a fixed income.

2011   15 July: The first performance of *Wasted* takes place at the Latitude Festival in Henham Park, Suffolk.

6 August: Following the killing of Mark Duggan, a 29-year-old Londoner, by police on 4 August, riots break out across London and quickly spread to cities

all over England, including Manchester, Birmingham, Liverpool and Nottingham. There is widespread arson and violence, and looting of consumer goods. Despite Duggan's killing and the strain that austerity cuts are already putting on inner-city communities, the government and press unite to declare that the riots are politically unmotivated acts of feral, criminal violence. Tempest disagrees with the media narrative, suggesting the riots were indeed politically motivated:

> Basically, it made sense to me I think because I'm a Londoner. It seemed absolutely logical to be honest. There was nothing about what happened then that was surprising. The narrative that was spun about it in the press was that it was this a-political consumption-like spasm, that's absolute fucking nonsense.

2011 also sees a wave of political movements across the globe, including the 'Arab Spring' (a series of pro-democracy protests in countries including Egypt, Morocco, Tunisia and Syria) and Occupy Wall Street, an anti-capitalist occupation in New York (later adopted elsewhere in the world including in Amsterdam, Paris, London and Hong Kong).

2012   Summer: London hosts the Olympics. The slow regeneration of the city that has been happening since at least the New Labour urban development drive at the turn of the century continues apace. Investment in new building developments renders many of London's former working-class neighbourhoods almost completely unrecognizable.

Kate Tempest develops *Brand New Ancients*, an epic spoken word poem at the Battersea Arts Centre in London; in 2013 this work wins the Ted Hughes Award for innovation in poetry.

Context: History, Society, Politics

When we study plays it can be tempting to begin with explorations of plot and character: to think about the emotional arc of a story and how it connects with us on a human level. What it made us *feel*. *Wasted* is, of course, a human story, especially resonant in terms of its emphasis on loss and friendship. The play follows 25-year-old south-east Londoners Ted, Danny and Charlotte on the ten-year anniversary of their friend Tony's death. As they deal with their grief and contemplate how life has progressed in the decade since Tony died, the trio face the limitations of their own happiness and, partying into the night, they try to work out what they might want from the future. The 'wasted' of the play's title refers both to the state of the characters' 'wasted' youth and potential, as well as to the fact that they are 'wasted' (inebriated on alcohol and drugs) by the end of the play.

Our emotional responses to characters and situations on stage are often deep and lasting. This means we might think about the emotional effects (that is, how the performance makes us feel) as 'timeless'. In *Wasted* this timeless quality is evident in a number of central themes, particularly in its exploration of the transition between youth and adulthood, a universal experience that is often deeply unsettling and fraught with uncertainty and indecision. We can also see timeless elements in the play's treatment of grief and loss, and in the central unresolved love story between Charlotte and Danny.

However, although *Wasted* has aspects that we might consider timeless, it also speaks very clearly to the social, political and historical moment in which it was written and performed. With an understanding of history and contemporary politics, we can map local, national and global events onto the play in order to help us think about it in a more focused, strategic way. Taking a step back like this – understanding the specifics of 'where, how and what' is on stage – can be a useful first step in the process of analysis, before we think about the meaning or emotional resonance of the work in general terms. Understanding context helps us to consider how performances work not only as entertainment, but as social and historical documents (situated in a specific time and place) that comment upon the world they are part of.

In the CHRONOLOGY section at the start of this volume I lay out a timeline with quite a detailed account of local, national and global events leading up to and following the first performance of *Wasted* in 2011. At first glance these may seem random in their selection: the evolution of hip hop in the Bronx, New York and its adoption into UK popular culture; the 1984–5 Miners' Strike; shifting political power in the UK; the birth of the millennial generation; the rise of neoliberalism; urban regeneration; the War on Terror; the 2011 UK riots and the decision to stage the Olympics in London. But, as I indicate in the header of the CHRONOLOGY section, these historical events, ostensibly unrelated, converge in *Wasted* in numerous ways. Although they are not directly addressed, these events sit underneath the narrative, shaping the social conditions that make the play possible and providing contexts that we can use to interpret what happens on stage.

The chorus, for example, draws on oral traditions rooted in hip hop culture (see the FORM AND GENRE section of this introduction). It uses the actors' 'real' voices to confront issues of millennial crisis, drawing attention to the hopeless, resigned state of a youth who are worse off than their parents' generation, and have no means of changing their reality. As the actors narrate towards the end of Chorus One:

Two   We realised,

One   This is all there is.

Three   There really isn't more.

One   Staring down the barrel

Two   Of an empty bottle

Three   Asking it to give us

All   More.[1]

Earlier generations – for example the hippies of the 1960s, the punks of the 1970s and 1980s, and the Free Party ravers of the 1990s – demonstrated their dissatisfaction with the status quo through identifiable movements, characterized by distinct styles and politics. These youth cultures often expressed counter-cultural ideals and acted directly and with urgency against prevailing social norms. What we see in *Wasted,* however, is a youth culture mired in a sense of hopelessness, with the characters unable to imagine or facilitate a life outside of the status quo. They are living in a bland, apolitical hedonism (chasing drink, drugs, romantic relationships, travel), and are ultimately trapped by work and the need to work. Interestingly this is even the case for Danny, who doesn't have a regular job, but is trying to 'make it' with his band. In Scene Three, he tells Ted he can't join Charlotte travelling because he is waiting for his big break ('we got this gig next week. You know, a big one. Might be some labels there').[2] Although it is suffocating him, the promise of commercial success proves too enticing to ignore.

The lack of an identifiable youth-driven politics in *Wasted* is perhaps symptomatic of a culture at large that has lost trust in political structures as a result of world events, exacerbated by an increasingly neoliberal environment. The events of 9/11, the resultant War on Terror (particularly the invasion of Iraq), and the 2008 financial crisis have deepened the sense both that politicians do not represent the interests of ordinary people, and that hoping for change is futile. This futility is suggested in the chorus (Chorus Two) as the actors stand on stage and tell the audience:

One   Change coming!

Two   Change coming!

One   I swear we can change something.

Three   We change nothing.

Two   Change is puffing up its chest.

One   Change is jumping to its death.

Three   Change is running,

One   Short of breath,

Two   Change is falling

Three   Change is calling on its people

Two   Change's people are not talking

One   Nothing changes.[3]

The repeated refrain 'change' in this hip hop style oration evokes the iconic track 'Changes', by American rapper Tupac. The academic Chris Richardson details how Tupac's lyrics might be read as a wail of despair that echoes out from the inner city, calling for help from those with the means to intervene.[4] We might read Tempest's chorus in the same way. Just as subway cars carried messages etched in graffiti from the Bronx into Manhattan,[5] the chorus brings the conditions of working-class London to the theatre, a traditionally elite cultural space. Indeed, at the start of the play the chorus draw attention to the fact we are in a theatre, emphasizing the disjuncture between this space and the lives depicted on stage. We might understand *Wasted* therefore as an attempt to reveal the conditions of those on the margins of society to those at the centre.

Throughout *Wasted* the characters struggle to 'change' – to break out of repetitive, soul-destroying routines. In many ways the play is a lamentation on the social order that sees working-class people relegated to the bottom of the pile. Although Ted, Charlotte and Danny are not traditional working-class, manual-labouring figures, they speak with local accents, and express their affiliation with those left out of mainstream culture through their words and actions. In Scene Two, for example, Charlotte, in her monologue to Tony, describes how she noticed a party of private school boys on a field trip as she travelled on a train into central London. She is struck by the stark difference between their lives and the lives of the children she teaches (presumably in south-east London). She describes how the boys from the private school spoke 'beautifully', looked healthy and easy in their own bodies; how they helped one another with algebra and French homework:

> it didn't seem fair. I thought of the kids here, in my class, with their squinty eyes and bad skin, mouths full of swear words and silence, and it didn't seem fair. And I'm stood there and I feel like bursting into tears and telling them all to run out on the streets and smash windows or something, do something.[6]

In this speech (and later when Danny refers to not having been to university[7]) there is a bubbling class politics, which hints at the injustices that neoliberalism, with its focus on individual success, has wrought on the working classes. Charlotte's call to her students to 'do something' is optimistically futile when we consider how attempts by the working-class to 'do something' about the conditions of their existence have played out in the recent past (for example, during the UK industrial strikes of the 1980s, which all but destroyed the strength of the trade unions), and the way that neoliberal politics and subsequent austerity measures have produced worsening conditions for the poorest in society.

Charlotte's statement is also prophetic. Three weeks after the first performance of *Wasted* in 2011, riots broke out in London and across England. These riots revealed simmering race and class tensions. The images and videos of the riots, documented in news media and still available on internet platforms such as YouTube, demonstrate exactly how disenfranchised youths took to the streets and smashed windows in an attempt to 'do something' about the unfairness of their lives. Tempest's ability to predict this event reveals how her writing is embedded in its social and historical context, reflecting the atmosphere of the world it represents.

Wasted takes place in a London that is rapidly undergoing transformation via urban development. Again, moments in the play that deal with this context point both to the specific period in which it was written, and predict changes that happen after the first performance. In Scene One, for example, Danny invites Ted to a party. Ted, sarcastically guessing what the party will be like, describes a 'warehouse in Peckham full of wannabe rude boys out to rob phones, and trendy fuckin' art students passed out in the corner experiencing Ketamine'.[8] This description draws on tropes of what the sociologist Ruth Glass called 'gentrification'.[9] Gentrification describes how formerly working-class neighbourhoods become fashionable, inhabited by artists and students before attracting developers who price out existing residents. Eventually, once working-class neighbourhoods become dominated by the middle classes, as poorer residents are displaced or forced elsewhere (a process that has accelerated in London since the 2012 Olympics, and has been called 'social cleansing'). The 'warehouse' Ted imagines the party taking place in is typical of the kind of trendy, pop-up social venues that began to spring up in areas like Peckham in the run-up to the London Olympics. The term 'pop-up' refers to an enterprise such as a café, shop, restaurant, bar or club, that makes temporary, often creative, use of a disused urban building.[10] These venues made Peckham and other districts that had previously been considered run-down (notably Hackney in east London) attractive to investors, who often built properties hoping to lure buyers seduced by the new nightlife and culture. Ted's animosity towards the 'warehouse' venue points to Tempest's cynicism towards this kind of speculative investment; one that has changed the face of London in the years since *Wasted* was written. Indeed, this is a theme Tempest has returned to in later works. On the album *Let Them Eat Chaos* (2016), for example, the song 'Perfect Coffee' describes the feeling of being alienated from your home environment in the wake of urban regeneration and investment that has destroyed everything familiar. The writer and performer Arinzé Kene also explores the effects of gentrification in his play *Misty* (Bush Theatre 2018).[11]

Despite the very human story at the heart of *Wasted*, then, it is nonetheless a play that we can read contextually. By mapping significant political, cultural and historical events onto the world of the play we begin to understand how its contents emerge in conversation with the wider world. This allows us a better understanding both of the play itself and of the human impact of the events that contextualize it.

Form and Genre

In *Wasted*, Tempest juxtaposes two stylistic forms: the chorus and the realistic or 'naturalistic' scenes. In doing this, she plays with a number of contemporary and historical literary and performance techniques, including poetry, direct address to the audience, monologues and dramatic scenes with two or three characters.

What we call 'form' describes the elements that give shape to a play (or piece of literature or music) and, together with content, places it in a particular genre. The formal juxtapositions of *Wasted* mean the play sits across a number of genres (or categories), most significantly hip hop, verse drama and realism (or 'naturalism'), discussed in more detail below. These elements work separately and together to create meaning, and connect the play to different contemporary and historical moments.

Hip hop

Kate Tempest is, first and foremost, a rapper. In an interview with me, she explained how a hip hop sensibility underpins all her writing. She is often referred to in newspapers and online reviews as a 'spoken word artist'; however, Tempest explains that she only began performing at so-called 'spoken word' events as a way to make money from her lyrics: 'I never defined myself [as a spoken word artist], and I never knew anyone else who I respected who defined themselves that way either.'

Choosing to define herself as a rapper, positioning her work clearly within the tradition of hip hop, is a political choice as well as a stylistic one. The term 'spoken word', as Conrad Murray, the director of the Battersea Arts Centre's Beatbox Academy has argued, decontextualizes rap from its social and political roots, sanitizing it for the kind of literary and cultural elite who attend events at theatres and art galleries.[1]

Hip hop is as much a cultural political movement as it is a popular commercial form: rooted in the experiences of those who are marginalized from society by virtue of their race and/or socio-economic status. Hip hop is deeply embedded in models of collective action and being together, or what hip hop practitioners call 'oneness'.[2] The 'cypher' (or 'cipher'), for example, demonstrates how this concept translates into practice: a cypher in hip hop is a circle in which a group of artists gather to share lyrics and dance moves or to jam together. Tempest explained to me that this form of sharing helps foster a commitment to what she calls 'improvement', a word that suggests both the way it encourages artistic development of the form itself, and the way the sharing-circle creates a vision for an improved world.

Appreciating Tempest's background in hip hop becomes significant when thinking about the function of the chorus in *Wasted*. Here the rhyming, poetic lyrics serve as a means by which the actors, stripped of their individual characters, epitomize 'oneness'. (Note how the stage directions specify that during the chorus actors are '*all and none of the characters*', and that they should '*speak in their own accents*'.[3])

The Chorus are a collective; it is only when they speak together that they can address the audience directly, with profound truths the characters cannot express. Juxtaposed with the realism of the preceding scenes, there is a sense that the chorus becomes holy – the 'something real' that the characters long to touch (see Chorus Three).[4] In this way the form offers us hope that we don't find in the plot, as the chorus demonstrates the 'different possibility for communication' that the characters are unable to imagine for themselves.

Verse drama

The term 'verse drama' refers to plays that are written with a metrical rhythm (they often, but not always, rhyme). Famous historical examples include the blank (non-rhyming) verse of Ancient Greek theatre, and the Early Modern verse pioneered by Shakespeare, often presented in a metrical composition called 'iambic pentameter'.[5] It is tempting to think of hip hop and classical forms of verse drama as totally separate genres. This is because verse drama is associated with what we think of as 'high' cultural history, and often sits in elite cultural spheres that seem vastly removed from the contemporary street-level appeal of hip hop. But hip hop is, as theatre scholar Harry Elm writes, 'a new form of cultural expression' that 'still retains, repeats, and revises the past as it pushes into the future'.[6]

Rapper and cultural critic Akala has argued that hip hop is actually closely connected to ancient and historical forms of oral storytelling, both in Europe and Africa. He points out the similarities between hip hop and Shakespeare in terms of poetic expression, experimental use of imagery and metre.[7] Akala also notes how the oration style developed by the hip hop emcee or 'rapper' draws on West African traditions of oral storytelling rooted in the figure of the *griot*, who used song, poetry and music to comment upon society, and often level political criticism.[8]

Wasted plays with the hip hop tradition of calling on historical forms of expression. Tempest's chorus, which as I argue above can be understood in terms of its hip hop context, also clearly draws on the ancient theatrical choral tradition. In Greek theatre, the chorus was a group of performers with no clear, distinctive individual identity, who commented upon the action of the play. As writer Kris Haamer explains, the Greek chorus had a number of functions, including 'creating a more meaningful connection between actor and audience'; allowing the playwright to create 'literary complexity'; and controlling the tempo of the play in order to 'prepare audiences for certain key moments in the storyline'.[9]

We see all three of these elements of the Greek chorus working through *Wasted*'s Chorus. The characters are introduced as a homogenous, ethereal group with no clear identity. They speak to the audience, acknowledging the theatrical construction by pointing out that this is a play, taking place in the theatre; as such we can read their subsequent statements as comments upon the play's action. The rhythm and metaphors spoken by the Chorus add literary complexity. The Chorus also changes the pace as we move between scenes: here Tempest is deftly controlling the audience experience, moving us into a state of thoughtful contemplation before the next 'realist' scene.

Tempest also calls on past theatrical traditions through the use of long monologues in each of the scenes, which have some parallels with the Shakespearean soliloquy. In these moments, although the characters do not speak with the sense of omnipotent 'truth' enabled by the Chorus, they do reveal elements of their inner lives that they are reluctant to show one another. The monologues are also not quite a direct address to the audience as Shakespearean soliloquies tend to be. Rather, they are delivered to Tony, the absent friend. In this way Tempest upholds the naturalistic world of the 'scenes', while exposing the fragility the characters find hard to share with one another.

Tempest's playful juxtaposition of historical dramatic and contemporary forms is not limited to *Wasted*. Several of her other works, in various forms, particularly poetry, play with the ancient and the new in similar ways. In the epic performance poem *Brand New Ancients* (Battersea Arts Centre 2012), for example, Tempest brings the myths of the Greek gods to contemporary London. By narrating the stories of ordinary Londoners' lives within an overarching framework of the mythical, she imbues what we might first think of as mundane with a sense of the profound and holy. Her collection of poems, *Hold Your Own*, meanwhile, uses the character of Tiresias, a gender-shifting clairvoyant from Greek mythology, as a recurring figure who frames an exploration of contemporary culture.

Realism/naturalism

The terms 'realism' and 'naturalism' are often conflated. Certainly they are related – both are artistic movements that emerged in the nineteenth century. Both movements sought to present real life, in as accurate detail as possible, although naturalism was often more concerned with 'environment' than realism was. As the theorist Raymond Williams writes, the 'novelty' of naturalism was 'its demonstration of the *production* of character or action by a powerful natural or social environment'.[10]

In *Wasted*, the opening stage directions, which are unusually detailed in their descriptions, suggest the way the characters are 'produced' by their social environments. We see, in turn, each of the characters in their workplaces (Ted in an office, Charlotte in the staffroom of a secondary school; Danny, whose job is as a part-time musician, is at the tail end of a party). The stage directions offer an exaggerated realism, where cardboard cut-outs stand in for fellow humans. Ted's colleagues are described as 'blown up, monstrous versions' of themselves; Charlotte's have 'massive eyebrows, ears, lips'; Danny's party-mates are similarly 'monstrous' and 'massive'.[11] This exaggerated form highlights the characters' sense of feeling alone and out of place in the world they inhabit. These soulless work environments frame the action of the subsequent scenes, as the characters reveal their dissatisfaction and misery. The importance of these work environments in conditioning the characters' dissatisfaction is further emphasized at the end, when the opening motifs are repeated.

Each of the 'Scenes' in the play is presented in a realist dialogue. That is, the characters speak to one another in ways that are very similar to how people speak to one another in real life, and they are placed in recognizable social situations and environments. This realism suggests that the Scenes reflect 'real life', and also show us how the characters are trapped by their real lives, which are repetitive and mundane. We get a sense of this in the lead up to and at the party scene: the 'wasted' characters have been here before. So, too, the opening and closing motifs suggest the characters' endless and repetitive routines. As we are told in the Chorus, 'nothing changes'.

This sense of changelessness shifts momentarily towards the end of *Wasted*, with Charlotte's plans to break out of the routine of her life and travel the world. However, these plans are thwarted because she is 'wasted': even she cannot follow through with a life radically different to the one she is living now. When juxtaposed with the more hopeful Chorus, the sense of the characters in the Scenes being stuck in a permanent, soulless cycle of work and partying has the effect of drawing attention to the limits of realism itself. As many scholars[12] have pointed out, realism, by replicating what already exists, fails to challenge dominant orthodoxies and structures (such as capitalism, sexism, racism and so on) that create social inequalities. Tempest's Chorus, then, is not only a direct comment on the Scenes in terms of its content, but also in terms of its form: the poetic oneness of the Chorus demonstrates how life for the characters could be different from the lives portrayed in the naturalistic Scenes, if they could break out of their conditioned behaviour.

Themes

Thinking through themes can enable us to consider how the plays we are studying operate *intertextually*: that is, how they connect with other plays, performances and works of literature. In *Wasted*, Tempest's hybrid approach to form and genre (that is, her mixing of different forms and genres) means her work, as we have already seen, resonates across historical periods and connects with a range of other artistic works, despite being very much a product of its specific moment.

Loss

The figure of Tony, the lost friend, is present throughout *Wasted*. Tony's absence tinges the action with poignancy, and serves as a constant reminder of the mortality of the other characters. Knowing that their lives too will end makes their 'wasted' states all the more pitiful, and the need to change even more urgent. The ever-presence of death in our lives is a theme that has been explored extensively in literature, drama and elsewhere. Think of Shakespeare's *Hamlet*, in which the ghost of Hamlet's father haunts the play. His mother's warning to him in Act One, Scene Two, when she tells him to stop grieving his father, and reminds him that 'All that lives must die', imbues that play with a similar sense of the 'waste' that can come from dwelling in loss.

Hip hop, too, often deals with loss, particularly with the loss of friends gone too soon. In the popular 1997 release 'I'll be Missing You', for example, Puff Daddy (subsequently known as P. Diddy, Diddy and Puffy) and Faith Evans commemorate their lost friend, the rapper Notorious B.I.G, who was murdered earlier that year. Like the characters in *Wasted* they reminisce over times shared together, directly address their absent friend and describe how, although no longer alive, he is still present ('words can't express what you mean to me / even though you're gone, we're still a team').

Neoliberalism

The term 'neoliberalism' describes an advanced form of capitalism, characterized by free-market economics and the privatization of government provision of public services. Proponents of this model argue that it allows a growth in wealth for the richest, which will 'trickle down' to benefit all members of society. Those who oppose neoliberalism argue that, instead, it has created greater wealth disparity than ever, meaning that while a few people hoard massive wealth, huge numbers suffer as they struggle to meet the costs of living – or become trapped in soul-destroying routines. Critics also argue that neoliberal ideology promotes selfishness and exacerbates environmental degradation, as it consumes without replenishing and focuses on the success of the individual over the advancement of society at large.

Although *Wasted* does not address the crisis of neoliberalism directly and explicitly (plays that do this include Caryl Churchill's *Serious Money* (Royal Court 1987)[1] and Lucy Prebble's *Enron* (Chichester Festival Theatre 2009),[2] both of which look at the financial machinations of neoliberalism), it does reveal how the lives of those living under this unfair system play out. The Chorus particularly draws explicit attention to these conditions (showing us how the populace becomes 'steeped in pretence' as we navigate a system that has us 'stressing over bills to pay'[3]).

Many contemporary works of realism that deal with working-class people and environments draw attention to the injustices of neoliberalism in similar indirect ways – displaying the lives of those 'left out' in order to expose the brutality and unfairness of the current system. Gary Owen's play *Iphigenia in Splott* (Sherman Theatre 2015),[4] for example, shows us the life of Effie as she struggles to survive in her small Welsh town that shows all the signs of austerity: 'boarded up houses, NHS cutbacks and people too worn-out to care about those falling through the cracks'.[5] Like Tempest, Owen draws on Greek mythology (in classical myth, Iphigenia is sacrificed to appease the goddess Artemis) in order to critique the conditions of the modern world, and highlight how even seemingly contemporary systems connect with timeless human concerns.

Youth culture

The transition from adolescence to adulthood, as we see in *Wasted*, is fraught. In Scene One, Danny encapsulates the crisis of early adulthood when he tells Ted how reflecting on the loss of Tony has made him realize he has been wandering aimlessly, letting his dreams fall away. He has become the person he is as a result of his actions, rather than through choice. ('All the things you done, that's just what you done. You weren't even thinking. But now, suddenly it's made you who you are. You can't go back, can ya?'[6]) Although the characters in *Wasted* articulate a sense of hopelessness particularly tied up with the millennial moment, the struggle of finding your way as an adult in politically fraught times is, as I mention above, a universal human experience.

In Shakespeare's *Romeo and Juliet* the struggle to become an adult and break out of the expectations of family and society end in tragedy. Jim Cartwright's 1986 play *Road* (Royal Court Theatre 1986),[7] on the other hand, is a seminal example of a social realist play that, like *Wasted*, explores how young people survive in times of social and political turmoil. It hones in on the young people on an unnamed road in Lancashire and records, 'with exemplary honesty, the consequences of living in an economically run-down society'.[8]

The 2016 play *We Are Ian* (Edinburgh Fringe), a devised piece by the collective In Bed With My Brother, similarly explores the theme of transitioning to adulthood. In this production, three figures on the cusp of adulthood in the mid-2010s listen to the disembodied voice of a character called 'Ian', who tells them how exciting it was to be part of the rave youth movement back in 1989. Bewildered and politically adrift, the trio attempt to recreate Ian's nostalgic rave stories, hilariously illustrating how little the millennial generation have to hold on to politically, utterly let down by a broken political system that is indifferent to their distress. The plays I mentioned above resonate with *Wasted* in both the 'timeless' ways they engage with the condition of becoming an adult, as well as, in the case of *Road* and *We Are Ian* especially, in how they interrogate the way contemporary political structures shape how young people are able to live their lives.

First Production

Wasted was first performed at the Latitude Festival, which is an annual music event that takes place at Henham Park, a sprawling country estate and former hunting ground in Suffolk, England. The production then toured the UK. Music festivals have become significant features of contemporary youth culture. Performance scholar Kathleen ('Alice') O'Grady has written about the potential of the festival site for fostering connection and creating a space for playful exploration.[1] She demonstrates how contemporary music festivals emerged from the Free Party scene of the 1980s and 1990s, associated with hedonism, drug taking and political activism (contemporary festivals also have their roots in the youth-driven festivals of the 1960s and 1970s in both the US and UK; Woodstock and Glastonbury being important historical examples). Music festivals today still retain traces of this radical history. Although the content of *Wasted* can be thought about in terms of the 'hopeless millennial' moment, then, we could also look at this specific first production and think about how the festival site connects the play to histories of radical youth movements – further emphasizing its 'youth culture' theme.

Plays make meaning not just through what is on stage and in the text, but also through where and how they are performed. Importantly, we can 'read' meanings onto the works we are analysing, using them to think more deeply about issues that might only be tangential to the plot or content of the plays themselves. In other words, plays don't only mean one thing. What we understand about what we see on stage depends on our own experiences, thought processes and points of view.

Perhaps then we can see *Wasted* as more hopeful when it is performed in a festival environment. Or perhaps we can think about how the world of 'wasted' young people on stage reflects the world of the festival and turns a mirror back on the audience. Another reading might be made in thinking about how festivals themselves, which were once radical anarchic sites, have been co-opted by corporate sponsors – what does the hopeless capitalist routine of wasting life in soulless corporate environments and trying to escape through drugs and alcohol have to say to us about the corporate sponsored festival? How can we make sense of a drama that is critical of the capitalist system, at a festival taking place on a country manor estate, the symbolic space of the landed gentry, bound up in the history of the UK's oppressive class system?

In the first production of *Wasted*, a large screen was used to project images, such as the opening motifs, to the audience. This illustrates one way in which a directorial choice was made that differs to the stage directions in the printed text. We might understand this decision too as a comment on contemporary youth culture, with the escalation of screen media via the use of mobile phones then (in 2011) a fairly recent development, as Tempest explained to me in an interview:

> *Wasted* came at the tail end of a time where things were on the cusp of changing. Things really, really changing. I think what I mean is the prevalence of information, the surge in the availability of new and social media, and the addictive nature of the smartphone as it gets more common to have one. Suddenly there's this attachment to phones.

While the characters themselves do not have smartphones (that, as Tempest also pointed out to me, would be impossible were she to write the play in 2018, when our interview takes place), the screen itself seems to comment on the ever-presence of the screen in contemporary life, and invites questions about how the experience of millennial youth is mediated via the screens.

Another interesting aspect of a production to 'read' in multiple ways is its casting. In the play text, *Wasted*'s characters are specified only by their names and ages (never specifically indicated, but suggested through the dialogue). They have no other defining features, aside from the London dialect they speak in. In the first production of *Wasted* all the actors were Caucasian (white). This affects how we might understand the play's politics, particularly in terms of its engagement with hip hop, which is a black cultural movement that emerged on the streets of New York. What does it mean for white actors to channel this history in a culturally elite space like the theatre? And how might the play's politics appear different if we cast actors of different races in the roles? Would this change the meaning? We can ask the same questions about gender – what if Charlotte, Ted or Danny were played by an openly transgender actor, for example? Does this, or could this, layer the play with alternative readings? These questions do not have definitive answers, but I offer them to encourage you to think about how performances work not only through what is written on the page, but through what appears on the stage – where, how and at what point in history.

Further Exploration

Works by Kate Tempest

Broken Herd, CD box set, Moresounds Lab (2009).
Best Intentions, EP with Sound of Rum, Bratwell Recordings (2009).
Patterns, self published poetry booklet (2010).
Balance, album with Sound of Rum, Sunday Best Recordings (2011).
Everything Speaks in its Own Way, poetry zine (London: Zingaro, 2012).
Brand New Ancients, epic performance poem (London: Picador, 2013).
Everybody Down, album, Big Dada (2014).
Hold Your Own, poetry collection (London: Picador, 2014).
Hopelessly Devoted, play (London: Methuen Drama, 2015).
The Bricks that Built the Houses, novel (London: Bloomsbury, 2016).
Let Them Eat Chaos, album (Kate Calvert Records, 2016).
Running Upon the Wires, poetry collection (London: Picador, 2018).

On Kate Tempest

Beswick, Katie. 'Build a Fortress', *Loud and Quiet*, 30 September 2015, https://www.loudandquiet.com/interview/kate-tempest/ [accessed 11 February 2019].

Lynskey, Dorian. 'Kate Tempest: "I engage with all of myself, which is why it's dangerous"', *Guardian*, 30 April 2017, https://www.theguardian.com/culture/2017/apr/30/kate-tempest-i-engage-with-all-of-myself [accessed February 2019].

McConnel, Jill. ' "We are still mythical": Kate Tempest's *Brand New Ancients*', *Arion* 22, no. 1 (2014): 195–206.

On hip hop

Forman, Murray. *The 'Hood Comes First: Race, Space and Place in Rap and Hip Hop* (Middletown, CT: Wesleyan University Press, 2002).

Hancox, Dan. *Inner City Pressure: The Story of Grime* (London: William Collins, 2018).

Kitwana, Bakari. *Why White Kids Love Hip Hop: Wankstas, Wiggers, Wannabes, and the New Reality of Race in America* (New York: Basic Civitas, 2005).

Rose, T. *The Hip Hop Wars* (New York: Basic Civitas, 2008).

Wood, A. ' "Original London style": London Posse and the Birth of British Hip Hop', *Atlantic Studies* 6, no. 2 (2009): 175–90.

On realism/naturalism

Fisher, Mark. *Capitalist Realism: Is There No Alternative?* (Ropely: Zero Books, 2009).

Innes, Christoper. *A Sourcebook on Naturalist Theatre* (London: Routledge, 2000).

Lay, Samantha. *British Social Realism: From Documentary to Brit Grit* (London: Wallflower, 2002).

Vanden Heuvel, Michael. 'Complementary Spaces: Realism, Performance and a New Dialogics of Theatre', *Theatre Journal* 44, no. 1 (1992): 47–58.

Williams, Raymond. 'A Lecture on Realism', *Screen* 18, no. 1 (1977): 61–74.

On gentrification

Harris, Andrew. 'Art and Gentrification: Pursuing the Urban Pastoral in Hoxton, London', *Transactions of the Institute of British Geographers* 37, no. 2 (2012): 226–41.

Lees, Loretta, Tom Slater and Elvin Wyly. *Gentrification* (London: Routledge, 2007).

Minton, Anna. *Big Capital: Who Is London For?* (London: Penguin, 2017).

Minton, Anna, Alberto Dumna, Malcolm James and Dan Hancox. *Regeneration Songs* (London: Repeater Books, 2018).

Pritchard, Stephen. 'Artwashing: Social Capital and Anti-
gentrification Activism', *Colouring in Culture*, 17 June 2017, http://
colouringinculture.org/blog/artwashingsocialcapitalantigentrification
[accessed 1 February 2018].

Notes

Context

1   Pages 32–33.
2   Page 62.
3   Pages 48–49.
4   Chris Richardson, 'Making "Changes": 2pac, Nas and the Habitus of the Hood', in *Habitus of the Hood*, ed. Chris Richardson and Hans A. Skott-Myhre (Bristol: Intellect, 2012), 193–214.
5   See CHRONOLOGY section of this introduction.
6   Page 44.
7   Pages 70–71.
8   Page 42.
9   Tom Slater, 'Gentrification of a City', https://www.geos.ed.ac.uk/ homes/tslater/gotcbridgewatson.pdf [accessed 10 February 2019].
10   Jen Harvie, *Fair Play: Art, Performance and Neoliberalism* (Basingstoke: Palgrave Macmillan, 2013), 119–127.
11   Arinzé Kene, *Misty* (London: Nick Hern Books, 2018).

Form and Genre

1   Katie Beswick, *Social Housing in Performance: The English Council Estate On and Off Stage* (London: Methuen Drama, 2019), 111.
2   Christina Zanfagna, 'Under the Blasphemous W(RAP): Locating the "Spirit" in Hip-Hop', *Pacific Review of Ethnomusicology* 12 (2006), https://ethnomusicologyreview.ucla.edu/journal/volume/12/piece/507 [accessed 10 February 2019].
3   Page 28.
4   Pages 65–66.
5   The term 'iambic pentameter' describes a line of verse, usually with ten syllables, where the speaker stresses the beat on every second syllable. For example, 'But, *soft*! what *light* through *yon*der *win*dow *breaks*?'
6   Harry Elm, 'Revising the Past, Pushing into the Future', *American Theatre* (2004), quoted in Nicole Hodges Persley, 'Hip-Hop Theatre and Performance', in *The Cambridge Companion to Hip-Hop* (Cambridge: Cambridge University Press, 2015), 85–98.

7   'Hip hop and Shakespeare? Akala at TEDXAldeburgh', *TEDXTalks*, YouTube, https://www.youtube.com/watch?v=DSbtkLA3GrY [accessed 7 February 2019].

8   Ibid.

9   Kris Haamer, 'The Function of the Chorus in Greek Drama' (2019), http://krishaamer.com/function-chorus-greek-drama/ [accessed 7 February 2019].

10   Raymond Williams, *Culture and Materialism* (London: Verso, 1980), 127.

11   Page 27.

12   See, for example, Michael Vanden Heuvel, 'Complementary Spaces: Realism, Performance and a New Dialogics of Theatre', *Theatre Journal* 41, no. 1 (1992): 47–58.

Themes

1   Caryl Churchill, *Serious Money* (London: Methuen Drama, 2002).

2   Lucy Prebble, *Enron* (London: Methuen Drama, 2009).

3   Page 33.

4   Gary Owens, *Iphigenia in Splott* (London: Oberon Books, 2015).

5   Tom Wicker, 'Iphigenia in Splott review at the National's Temporary Theatre London – "blisteringly powerful"', *The Stage*, 30 January 2016, https://www.thestage.co.uk/reviews/2016/iphigenia-in-splott-review-at-the-nationals-temporary-theatre-london-blisteringly-powerful/ [accessed 11 February 2019].

6   Page 39.

7   Jim Cartwright, *Road* (London: Samuel French, 2014).

8   Michael Billington, 'Road review – raucous look back at a divided Britain still hits home', *Guardian*, 30 July 2017, https://www.theguardian.com/stage/2017/jul/30/road-review-royal-court [accessed 10 February 2019].

First Production

1   Kathleen O'Grady, 'Dancing Outdoors: DiY Ethics and Democratised Practices of Well-being on the UK Alternative Festival Circuit', *Dancecult: Journal of Electronic Dance Music Culture* 7, no. 1 (2015): 76–96.

Wasted

Wasted premiered at Latitude Festival on 15 July 2011 and the cast was as follows:

Ted   Alexander Cobb

Danny   Ashley George

Charlotte   Lizzy Watts

The play toured in 2012 to twenty-six venues. The role of Ted was played by Cary Crankson and the role of Danny by Bradley Taylor.

Direction James Grieve
Design Cai Dyfan
Lighting Design Angela Anson
Sound Design Tom Gibbons
Music Kwake Bass
Film Design Mathy Tremewan and Fran Broadhurst

A blank line of speech indicates a character does not have the words.

These stage directions are open for interpretation.

Dark stage. Sounds of London play out the speakers. Drunks singing. Sirens. Market men. Television hosts heard through living room windows. Traffic. People laughing. School kids screaming. All field recordings, actual London sounds. Projections of London play on the screen. Lights come up gently, like sunrise, revealing each character one at a time.

Ted *is at a shitty little desk, really small, with a massive phone on it and a chunky old computer monitor and loads of files. He looks like he feels sick. He is smiling politely. To either side of him are cardboard cut-outs of middle-aged women with immaculate hair, something about them is hideous. They have oversized heads. They are blown up, monstrous versions of work colleagues. The sounds now are of phones ringing, call centre type voices, not clearly saying anything, but polite, sickly tones, pretending to be helpful, also women talking about celebrity couples, their next door neighbours. Mindless gossip. Teddy stares straight ahead.*

Charlotte *is in the staff room. Sounds of boiling kettles, laughing teachers, inaudible bullshit conversation. The tones are sarcastic, tired. People show off and compete for the upper hand. The conversations are dominated by exaggerated bellowing, the arsehole teacher slagging off the kids to make themselves feel better. Bells ringing. Photocopier sounds. Charlotte stands between two cardboard cut-outs of teachers with massive eyebrows, ears, lips, a woman in drab clothes – ill fitting leggings type – and a balding man in glasses and liverspots. Charlotte is smiling along, but looks like she might faint, or cry, or something. She looks completely alone, despite all the noise.*

Danny *is sitting on a dingy sofa, in front of a coffee table. Power ballads playing from a cheesy radio station. Magic FM.[1] Bullshit conversation, sound of loud, exaggerated sniffing, people doing lines. To either side of him are two cardboard cut-outs of 25-year-old London men, they are both wearing very similar jeans and t-shirts. They are bulky. Their heads are monstrous, especially their* *nostrils and mouths. Also two women, laughing hysterically, massive eyelashes, lips, perfect hair. Over-exaggerated laughing. Inaudible*

retelling of teenage memories. Empty cans of lager and bottles of strange spirits – weird things like chocolate liqueur and Babycham.[2] Anything goes at this time of the morning. The voices in the room are talking over each other, singing along to the power ballads, laughing. **Danny** *looks sick, like the other two have looked, confused, but he's smiling and nodding along. Cutting up a line for himself.*

The sound swells to uncomfortably loud, maybe some white noise, and then cuts out. These three, as well as being the characters, are also the **Chorus***. When they are speaking the Chorus lines, they are all and none of the characters. Any of them can speak any of the Chorus lines. They should speak to the audience. They shouldn't be afraid of smiling at the audience, or looking at them dead in the eye. They should speak in their own accents, and be aware of the meter beneath the words, in the way that you are aware of a beat when you dance to a song. These are not the characters yet (even though they are) they are also everyone that's ever felt how the characters feel.*

Chorus One

One   If we're being honest with you,

Three   Actually honest, not just apparently honest.

One   Then we have to tell you, we don't have a clue what any of you are doing here.

Two   We're not really sure what any of us are doing here.

Three   Thing is,

Two   We wish we had some kind of incredible truth to express.

One   We wish we knew the deeper meaning.

Three   But we don't.

Two   We don't have nothing to tell you that you don't already know, and we thought it was worth acknowledging that.

Three   Fuck it, while we're speaking plainly, let's get it all out in the open.

One   We're not used to this kind of environment.

Two   We're the people that feel awkward in theatres,

One   The people that don't laugh at the bits where everyone else laughs.

Two   The people that never know what to say afterwards when everyone else is expressing their opinions.

Three   We don't want to stand here in front of you and pretend we can't see you.

One   We can see you.

Three   You look lovely. And we're glad you're here.

One   We are.

Two   We don't want to show you something impressive that makes you feel clever.

One   No.

Three   We just want to show you something honest,

One   Something ours.

Two   And we'll be happy if it makes you feel anything at all.

One   No big deal, but

Three   At the same time,

One   Everything we ever knew.

Two   What this is, is home.

One   Deserted playgrounds, tramps singing on the street, bleeding gums outside the pub, takeaways and car exhausts and bodies till you can't see bodies.

Three   Working shit jobs

Two   And trying to care about things you don't care about

Three   And saving up to buy things you hate yourself for wanting.

All   Home.

Two   A city where nothing much happens except everything.

Three   Where everyone is so entirely involved in their own

One   'nothing much'

Three   That they forget about the everything happening elsewhere.

Two   And the thing is, if we're being honest with you,

One   And that's all we want to be –

Two   It's important that we tell you that we have no idea what we're doing.

One   We need you to understand the history here.

Three   See –

One   We were thirteen once, with our fists full of beer that we jacked[3] from the offie,

Three   We lived without fear.

Two   We looked up to our elders,

Three   And awaited the days

Two   When we'd be looked up to by kids half our age.

Three   The years passed,

One   We got wasted in raves and felt

Two   Godlike.

Three   Held spliffs[4] up in the dark of the party like

Two   Fog lights.

One   We were children in a city of

Two   Dogfights and rock pipes,[5]

One   Surrounded by

Two   Deadbeats and lost types

Three   London belonged to

All   Us

Two   We smoked skunk[6] on the bus.

Three   Everything was ours.

One   We got thumped in the guts but

All   Stood firm.

Three   We was young and we trusted each other,

Two   It was all romantic and real.

Three   We was frantic and full of our feelings and laughing and squealing,

One   Holding our sides beneath the unfolding of skies in the evening.

Two   Ah, but things happened.

Three   Our eyes got

One   Dimmer

Three   And our dreams got

One   Flattened.

Two   We got older, didn't we? We got responsibilities,

One   Started seeing our defiance as arrogance and stupidity.

Two   We used to be rebellious

Three   And angry

One   And in it all together,

Three   But time passed and we realised

Two   Nothing

One   Lasts

Three   Forever.

Two   So now we carry it within us, the fact we used to be

One   Eternal,

Two   Before the world caught up and we forgot what we was living for.

Three   We became

One   The inmate,

Two   The guard,

Three   And the key that locked the prison door.

Two   We used to skim the surface

One   Till we sank and hit the river floor.

Two   We realised,

One   This is all there is.

Three   There really isn't more.

One   Staring down the barrel

Two   Of an empty bottle

Three   Asking it to give us

All   More.

One   Hearts beating

Three   Slower than they used to, stressing over bills to pay,

Two   A million distractions just to fill the day,

Three   Faces greyer than before. It's not our world no more

One   It's someone else's.

Two   We're less empathetic and more

Three   Selfish,

Two   Less independent and more

Three   Helpless.

Two   Thing is though,

One   We soldier on through the cityscape,

Two   Trying to carve out a niche for ourselves in our little ways.

Three   Life's great,

One   Life's awful.

Two   Repetitions and figure eights,

One   We're living like our best days

Two   Have already slipped away.

One   And honestly,

Three   How can we rise up and take the reigns back,

Two   When all we really wanna do is to kill our dreams and let our brains

All   Smack

Two   Themselves about in the corner of a rave?

Three   Desperate for someone to help us, but convinced we can't be saved.

One   We got friends we known since we were born, but we can't tell them what we're feeling,

Three   We're alone with the city in all its dirty heaving mess –

Two   Where the children fight for breath and get old before their time,

One   Or, die young enough to live forever, or lose their fuckin' minds.

Three   And that's the perfect tragedy of London –

Two   A city where the best of us lose our ability to function,

One   And the worst of us thrive,

Two   And the rest of us stride on and on through

Three   The mess,

Two   The rust,

Three   The flesh,

Two   The lust,

Three   The lies.

One   The breath,

Three   The dust,

One   The skies we lift our heads to watch,

Three   The pride.

Two   The sex,

Three   The blood,

Two   The fried food,

Three   The stress

Two   The way we hide from the truth that is inside.

Three   We hold so tight to our disguise,

One   That we find ourselves alone when we're surrounded, divided from our tribe.

Scene One

Ted *is sitting on a park bench looking out at the audience. He's looking at Tony's tree. He has a can in his hand, a plastic bag full of cans by his feet. He's wearing a cheap suit and shoes, but he doesn't look shabby. He looks smart. Smoking. He sits there for a long moment before speaking. Sound of birds, distant sirens. Kids screaming in a playground somewhere. Traffic.* **Ted** *seems quite pissed.[7] But he's holding it together.*

Ted   It used to be, we hung out coz I couldn't wait to be around her, couldn't wait to bury my head in her tits and listen to her giggle. But now. Now, we wake up together every morning and it don't feel the same.

I think I'm miserable, Tony. I wouldn't want her to know that, it don't seem fair on her, but between you and me mate, I think I'm pretty fuckin' miserable. Right now I mean, today.

She thinks I'm on the career ladder coz I wear this shitty suit to the office, but I'm not though, Tony, I'm going nowhere, surrounded by idiots. Nicole from accounts, stinkin' of custard creams[8] and talkin' all the fuckin' time. Mate. It's killin' me, the weeks go by, every day the same shit. I'll be doin' the stock take and the data entry 'til I'm dead in the ground and it won't have made the slightest bit of difference to no one. I wouldn't even mind it, you know, it's work. It's payin' the bills, but it's so fuckin' tedious though. I'm in there, all day, giving them all of my fuckin' time, and every day that goes past stacks up, and I swear it, right, sometimes, at night, I can see all the days I've given 'em, all huddled together in this massive crowd at the foot of my bed, laughin' at me when I'm trying to sleep. We're still young, for fuck's sake. We could sell the car. Leave the flat. Fuck off for a year. We could live in Spain, I could get a job in a bar.

She could be a waitress. We could swim naked in the sea. We could get drunk in the afternoons and sleep it off on the beach, we could …

Danny *walks up the path behind him and stands next to him for a minute, looking at the bag by his feet. He sits down.*

Danny   Alright, Ted?

Ted   Alright, Dan?

Danny   How's it goin'?

Ted   Yeah, alright mate, not bad.

Danny *looks around, at the tree, smokes his cigarette.*

Ted   Ten years.

Danny   I know mate. Feels like yesterday, dunnit?

Ted   Feels like ten years to me.

Danny *takes some skunk out of his pocket and starts skinning up,[9] it's a bit windy. Without being asked to,* **Ted** *shields* **Danny***'s hand from the wind.*

Ted (*to* **Tony***, about* **Danny**)   He ain't changed much, still believes he can have whatever he wants. Thinks he's gonna play guitar on seminal albums and tour America and write a cult fuckin' novel that'll change the way we think about our lives. Shit. He's one of my oldest friends, and I love him to pieces. I'd lie down and fuckin' die in the road for him – but sometimes, sometimes, he can be a bit of a knob. You know, I'm not being funny, but, you know, when he's with all his cool new 'creative' mates. They ain't real, Tony. They ain't like us. They sit around, with ironic trousers on and three haircuts each, waiting to be discovered.

What he don't realise is that in ten years, he'll be thirty-five, one a them fuckers we used to laugh at at parties, gurning his face off, dribbling over some nineteen-year-old acid casualty called Sparkle telling himself he's still got it. He'll be there, giving it the old – I might be sensitive but I'm still dangerous – treating women like shit coz he hates himself for never having had the guts to put himself second and commit to one of 'em. It takes strength to commit, Tone, it really fuckin' does … Then, next thing he knows, he'll be forty-five, strung out from the cocaine and the booze and the MDMA,[10] having panic attacks every night when he's on his own, coz he'll have realised that he's too old to be young anymore, and the world won't apply to him, and all the kids'll be listening to music he don't understand and suddenly all o' them interesting ideas he had, and all them exciting collaborations he was involved in, won't be half as fuckin' important anymore. He'll be worse off than me then. He'll have no seminal fuckin' work to wank off about, he'll be alone in his trendy flat, conducting imaginary interviews with imaginary journalists about imaginary masterpieces. And me? I'll be as miserable as I've always been, right there beside him.

Danny *finishes rolling the joint.*[11] *He lights it, lifts it to the tree, exhales, passes it to* **Ted. Ted** *smokes, heavily.*

Danny   What do you reckon he'd be up to now?

Ted   What d'you mean?

Danny   Like, for a job.

Ted   Dunno. Same as the rest of us probably. Fuck all.

Danny   Nah, he would have been something.

Ted   Like what?

Danny   I dunno. Something.

Ted   Like what?

Danny   Dunno. Chef. Have his own restaurant.

Ted   He couldn't cook an egg, mate.

Danny   Cameraman then. Or a vet or something. I dunno. Anything. Fuckin' lawyer.

Ted   Lawyer?

Danny   Fireman.

Ted   He would have made a good lawyer actually.

Danny   Train driver.

Ted   Know what I heard about train drivers?

Danny   What?

Ted   If you drive a train and you hit three people. Like, if three people jump out in front of your train.

Danny   Yeah?

Ted   You get paid leave and a pension rest of your life.

Danny   Really?

Ted   Yeah, even if you only been on the job a week.

Danny   That's mental.

Ted   Sounds alright though, don't it? I was thinking about doing it.

Danny   Yeah?

Ted   Couldn't handle it though, if someone did jump out.

Danny   Never forgive yourself would ya?

Ted   Three times as well. Fuck you right up that would.

Danny   Still, he woulda been something, Ted. He would have.

Ted   Well, we'll never know now, will we?

Danny   No. S'pose not.

Ted   Such a waste.

Pause. They drink.

Danny   How's work?

Ted   Yeah, it's alright.

Danny   Same old same old eh?

Ted   Something like that, yeah.

Danny   I dunno how you do it, mate.

Ted   Well, you just do, don't ya? You just do.

Danny Yeah, s'pose.

Ted What about you? How's the band and that?

Danny Oh yeah, great yeah. Well, you know, we don't have a drummer at the moment, but we have got these t-shirts we made. And I met a guy the other day who said he'd be up for drumming for us, and he's pretty good as far as I can tell. Well, I ain't heard him drum, but, he looks like a drummer. Long hair, tattoos and that. Nice guy.

Ted Tell you the truth, Dan, I can't fuckin' stand it.

Danny Can't stand what?

Ted It's not like you set out to end up nowhere is it.

Danny You ain't nowhere, mate. You're working hard.

Ted I need to change it up, Dan. If not for me, for him. I mean, look.

Danny What?

Ted Well, look at his tree.

Danny What about it?

Ted Even that changes four times a year. Know what I mean?

Danny Yeah, I do. I do. I been thinking the same thing.

Ted Course you have.

Danny Day like today, you think, fuck. Don't you? All of a sudden ten years has gone by. All the things you done, that's just what you done. You weren't even thinking. But now, suddenly it's made you who you are. You can't go back, can ya?

Ted No, you can't.

Danny So, I'm making some changes right now, as it goes. I had an epiphany, didn't I.

Ted An epiphany?

Danny Yeah, you know. Like a realisation.

Ted   Yeah, I know what it fuckin' means, mate. What did you realise?

Danny   That it's time, innit, it's time now.

Ted   Time for what?

Danny   Time for me to sort my shit out.

Ted   In what way?

Danny   In all ways. I've gotta fix up. Get a proper job, stop getting fucked all the time.

Ted   Why?

Danny   For Charlotte, innit.

Ted   Charlotte?

Danny   I want her back, don't I.

Ted   Serious?

Danny   Yeah.

Ted   How's that going then?

Danny   Well, it's up and down to be honest. Sometimes it feels like she's up for it, but then suddenly she goes all cold.

Ted   Well, she's probably just trying to be careful mate.

Danny   She's driving me mental.

Ted   Do you mean it?

Danny   Course I mean it. That's what I'm saying, I need to fix up.

Ted   She's a nice girl, Dan. She's not a dickhead.

Danny   I wanna settle down.

Ted   You wanna settle down?

Danny   Yeah. What's wrong with that?

Ted   You broke her heart, Dan.

Danny   I just need one more chance. That's all. If she'd just give me one more chance, it'd be different this time, but that's what I'm saying, you can't go back can ya?

Ted   No.

Danny   Like, last night, we went for a drink.

Ted   Yeah?

Danny   Fuckin' great it was. Went back to hers. It was all good. But then, like this morning, soon as I wake up she's giving me the silent treatment, looking at me like I tricked her or something. Like I done something bad, I say, what's going on, then she just freezes up, leaves for work.

Ted   That good was it.

Danny   I keep telling her, fresh start, but what can I do? If she's always expecting me to act the cunt, pretty soon, I'm gonna act the cunt, aren't I?

Ted   She needs to know you ain't gonna waste her time again. She's testing you.

Danny   I ain't gonna waste her time again, Ted. That's what I'm saying. The epiphany, it dawned on me, you know, today, Tony's day and all that. I got to stop pissing about and actually get something started. Show her innit. Show her that I mean it.

Ted   Yeah?

Danny   I'm changing things, ain't I, this is it, mate.

Ted   Well, good for you, pal. Good for you.

They drink. Smoke the spliff. **Danny** *takes a puff and holds the smoke in, passes it to* **Ted** *and doesn't exhale until he gets the joint back.* **Ted** *does the same.*

Danny   What you doing later anyway?

Ted   Dunno, this, more of this.

Danny   We should do something, shouldn't we? Celebrate.

Ted   Celebrate what? He's dead.

Danny   You know what I mean. Mark the occasion. He would have wanted us to.

Ted   What you got in mind?

Danny   Well, there's this party my mates are putting on.

Ted   What kind of party?

Danny   Nothing too mental,

Ted   Oh right, just the usual twenty rig sound clash then, let me guess – warehouse in Peckham[12] full of wannabe rude boys out to rob phones, and trendy fuckin' art students passed out in a corner experiencing Ketamine.[13] Think I'm alright, mate.

Danny   Don't be a dick. Come on.

Ted   What about your epiphany?

Danny   What about it?

Ted   It's not really my thing anymore, Dan.

Danny   It'll be a laugh.

Ted   A laugh? We'll get there, you'll fuck off and start chatting to a bunch of people with adjectives instead of names, while I sit there like a lemon, getting drunk on my own.

Danny   It won't be like that, Ted. Come on, we ain't been out in ages.

Ted   That's coz I ain't really on it no more.

Danny   Ten years, Ted. Come on, for Tony, mate.

Ted   Charlotte going?

Danny   Yeah, she is.

Ted   Maybe it would be nice, me and you and Charlotte, like the old days, eh?

Danny   Exactly.

Ted   Alright, let's go party then, shall we? But you can't just fuck off with her the minute we get there and leave me, Billy no mates, looking like someone's brought their Dad along.

Danny   Nah, Ted. The three of us. We'll go and have it, for Tony, and the old days. And for right now. And for fuckin' forever mate.

Ted   Oh stop will ya, I'm welling up.

Scene Two

Charlotte's *standing at a bar, with a gin and tonic. She looks tired. The cardboard cut-outs from earlier are all around her. Sound of people talking, not saying much, songs from a juke box, doors opening and closing, barmaid bantering with regulars. The friendly sounds make a contrast with the still, monstrous cut-outs, who are crowding her. Really close to her. She faces the audience, with them either side, the bar between her and the edge of the stage.*

Charlotte   I'm stood at the front of the class and I feel like I'm drowning. I'm staring out at them, and I'm thinking who the fuck are you lot anyway? I look at them, but I can't see children, I can just see the colour of their jumpers, smudges where their faces should be.

Behind me, today's date is written on the board. I'm trying to pretend I don't know what it means.

It's hot and the classroom stinks, and the clock's broken and the work stuck up on the walls is old and the corners are coming away and the kids are screaming.

I'm trying to remember why I wanted to do this in the first place. You can't inspire minds on a timetable like this.

I think I'm miserable, Tony.

I mean, I stand in the staffroom in between classes and smile along with the others, but they're all so bitter, Tony. They're all so fuckin' hateful. Thirty years in the job, and they hate everything about it, but it's too late for them to get a new job and I'm pretty sure that secretly they hope the kids'll come to nothing. I mean it. You should hear the way they talk about them. No wonder the kids are killing each other over postcodes,[14] or getting sick at the thought of not being famous.

The classroom's hot, and I'm staring at the kids, and I'm remembering us lot when we was at school – moving through the corridors like we was the fuckin' Roman empire. I'm remembering how it felt to be fifteen, us lot, in a party, feeling like the world was ours, like we fuckin' owned it. I'm remembering how we cared about each other, how we got in fights for each other and robbed Tescos[15] and built fires and got off our faces, it was exciting, wasn't it? It felt real.

What even happened to us? We go parties now, and we've got nothing to say to each other 'til we're fucked. And even then. We spend hours talking about parties from before, things that happened to us once, we spend life retelling life and it's pointless and boring.

And so, I'm staring out at the kids, watching them slouching in their chairs and playing with their phones and suddenly I'm remembering the other day, sunlight through the window of a hot train, I'm sat there, heading into town, and there's a group of ten or fifteen boys on some kind of field trip with their teacher, and they're wearing nice uniforms, they must have been from a private school or something. I mean, I listened to them talking to each other and I wanted to cry, coz these were young men with beautiful voices and healthy hair and good posture, talking to each other in perfect English, and helping each other with equations and fuckin' algebra and asking each other questions about how to say this or that particular thing in French, and it didn't seem fair. I thought of the kids here, in my class, with their squinty eyes and bad skin, mouths full of swear words and silence, and it didn't seem fair. And I'm stood there and I feel like bursting into tears and telling them all to run out on the streets and smash windows or something, do something. I want to tell them they're perfect and they're strong and tell them to go out and live every minute of their lives from their guts, to go after what they want, to own this fuckin' terrible city and get all they can out of life. But I don't say anything do I? I mean, what could I say?

I say nothing. I just stand there and listen to them telling each other to fuck off, I stare at the broken clock, the work peeling off the walls, and I know this is the last time I'll stand here in front of them, the last time. And I'm staring at them, wondering what they'll be like ten years from now. And then, suddenly, I'm thinking of Danny. I'm thinking of last night. It was perfect. But then I woke up and I looked at him, and I thought about the future. Six months down the line, a year maybe, two. I'll be distant, worn out by him, and he'll be pretending nothing's changed, out of pride he'll put his doubts away, convince himself to be this man he tells me only I can make him, this better man he talks about. But really, we'll be sick of each other, we'll be stifled and clinging to each other as tight as we can to keep ourselves from accepting there's nothing you can give a person that don't take half of them away. I can see myself, eating alone at the kitchen table, wondering where he is, the nagging girlfriend, uptight and unreasonable, his laughter in the pub, shrugging it off, me, sat there, feeling so self-righteous that even when he does come home I can't show him that deep down I'm really fuckin' happy to see him. And then the moody silences, and off to bed, and strange, private dreams, and waking up to the alarm going and kissing him goodbye without smiling and on and on until everything I want for myself is forgotten. Even if it feels good now, it'll end in the same grey routine, the cozy choking afternoons. The unsaid words getting heavier and heavier 'til we don't even fight out loud anymore.

And so here I am, in front of the class, and the classroom's hot and I feel like I'm drowning and I walk out of the classroom. I open the door and walk out of the classroom. And the kids are shouting after me, but I ignore them. I walk down the corridor, I turn left, I walk down the stairs, kids everywhere, I swim through them, turn left again, the doors. I walk through the doors. I'm in the air. I'm outside. It's raining gently. It's good. I'm walking to the bus stop. I'm leaving. I'm making a decision. I'm changing things. This is it.

And then I'm coming in here and I'm ordering a drink for me and one for you, Tony, and I'm carrying them over to the table in the corner, and I'm staring at the pint and the empty chair and I'm trying to remember the first time they served us in here. I'm taking a sip of my drink, and then I'm taking a sip of your drink. And I'm remembering your face, and I'm smiling to myself. It's the weekend, Tony, the first weekend of the rest of my life.

Ted (*like he might have said it a few times already*)   Charlotte?

Charlotte   Alright, Ted. Sorry, I was miles away.

Ted   Someone sitting here?

Charlotte   No, go on.

Ted   What, that not someone's drink?

Charlotte   Got it for, Tony. Silly innit?

Ted   No course not, not silly at all.

Charlotte   You been to his tree yet?

Ted   Yeah.

Charlotte   How was it?

Ted   Oh, you know, still there. You been down yet?

Charlotte   Nah, not yet. Couldn't face it. Came here instead.

Ted   How's work?

Charlotte   Yeah, it's alright. How's yours?

Ted   Yeah, ya know. Not bad.

Charlotte   I miss him, Ted. Do you? Do you miss him?

Ted   Yeah. Course I do.

Charlotte

Ted   But you know what?

Charlotte   What?

Ted   Of all the conversations we had, me and him, over the years and that, I can't remember any of 'em.

Charlotte   What d'you mean?

Ted   Like, we spent years talking to each other, but I can't remember a word we said.

Charlotte   Far as I remember it was mainly – safe bruv, heavy, or let me have a Rizla.[16]

Ted   Point is, you don't remember the particulars do you, just the feelings. I know I knew him, but I can't remember how. You know what I mean?

Charlotte   Not really.

Ted   That's why you got to act on your feelings innit, coz it's all you got. you're either happy, or you ain't.

Charlotte   I left my job.

Ted   What? Really? How?

Charlotte   I just handed my notice in.

Ted   What, that it? Just like that?

Charlotte   Yeah. I just walked out.

Ted   Fuck. You left your job! … How do you feel? Do you feel different?

Charlotte   No, not really, not yet.

Ted   So what you gonna do?

Charlotte   I'm going away.

Ted   What?

Charlotte   I ain't told anyone yet, but I booked a flight. I'm off, Ted.

Ted   What?

Charlotte   I just thought, fuck it, you know. Fuck it. And I went online, and I booked a flight and that's it, I'm leaving.

Ted   What about Danny?

Charlotte   What about Danny?

Ted   You tell me.

Charlotte   It's complicated.

Ted   Why?

Charlotte   I don't know.

Ted   Don't you like him?

Charlotte   No, not really, he's an arsehole.

Ted   Everyone needs an arsehole.

Charlotte   I don't trust him, Ted.

Ted   He means it this time.

Charlotte   He thinks he does. And he's very convincing, but I don't believe him. And I don't want to feel guilty for always doubting him.

Ted   What do you want then?

Charlotte   I just want a change.

Ted   Is that why you're going away?

Charlotte   Yeah.

Ted   When you gonna tell him?

Charlotte   I don't know

Ted   You coming out tonight though, right?

Charlotte   Well, I was gonna, but, I got to pack and

Ted   Nah Charlotte, you gotta come out girl. You gotta. For Tony and that. It'll be a right laugh. For me. And for Dan. The three of us. You gotta come. Anyway, packing can wait can't it. When you leaving?

Charlotte   Tomorrow.

Ted   Tomorrow?

Chorus Two

One   Change coming!

Two   Change coming!

One   I swear, we can change something.

Three   We change nothing.

Two   Change is puffing up its chest.

One   Change is jumping to its death.

Three   Change is running,

One   Short of breath,

Two   Change is falling.

Three   Change is calling on its people,

Two   Change's people are not talking.

One   Nothing changes. You walk around the city,

Two   Stare at strangers,

One   You might notice an expression on a friend you known for ages,

Two   But it's hopeless,

Three   We can't keep each other safe,

One   We can barely focus.

Three   We just want to live a little,

Two   And what's living if it doesn't kill you?

Three   Every atom in us screams at us to let our hearts out,

One   But it's easier to

Two   Pass out

One   Than to fall asleep peacefully.

Three   If we're lying to each other, we don't mean it deceitfully –

Two   We're nothing more than rag and bone,

One   We close our eyes

Three   And stagger home,

One   While the groaning timbers in the windows seem to brag and moan –

Three   They say, 'well, you look older

Two   But you haven't grown.'

One   We see our faces slide across the pane,

Three   We look away,

One   Nothing for it,

Two   Bosh your brain to glory,

Three   Same old story

One   And it shows no sign of

Three   Ending.

One   Coz there's a whole night ahead of us,

Two   Ours for the befriending,

Three   And no matter what our brains beg of us,

One   Our hearts are ripe for the tempting.

Three   See,

One   When you're sick of being trodden down

Three   You reach for your ascension in the nonsense that you swallow down.

Two   We just wanna find some

One   Substance

Two   In this hollow town.

One   It doesn't matter that tomorrow's round the corner if your sorrows drowned tonight,

Two   At least that's something,

One   And how can we be blamed when every day's the same?

Two   We just want to lose our names and our edges.

One   We just want to lose our minds

Three   And lose the lines that draw the borders.

Two   The shadows haunt the corners,

Three   No one's gonna laugh at you if no one knows you're tortured.

Two   We want to change,

One   But change aborted becomes strange

Three   And we are taunted by the same old repetitions,

Two   We grin,

One   But our smiles are contorted,

Three   And we forget our epiphany

One   The minute that we thought it.

Scene Three

*A party in a warehouse in Peckham. All three characters are
completely munted.*[17] *But not in a caricature kind of way. In a
way that suggests they've been getting munted for many years,
and know how to take drugs without having to make a big deal
out of it. Dark lit stage, maybe strobe lights, or UV strip lights
to make them look a bit monstrous, make their teeth look dirty,
eyes look a bit alien etc. Dirty bass music playing. Loud. Nothing
cheesy. Really dirty and bass heavy.*[18] *There should be a feeling of
loads of other people in the room. Maybe the cardboard cut-outs
from earlier.* **Danny** *and* **Ted** *are sitting together with their backs
against the speakers, on the floor, grinning, with their arms round
each other's necks looking a bit like they're ten years old. There
should be a massive difference in their physicality compared to
earlier when they were sat on the bench together. They should be
open and tactile. They giggle for a bit, then start wrestling each
other. The three of them are dancing, in their own worlds, and then
together.* **Ted** *throws his arms around both of their necks, they're*

all together, in a little love huddle, raving, and munted, looking up to the lights, swallowing, grinning, touching each other.

Blackout, sound stops. Lights come up and it's daylight, sickly kind of daylight that you never really want to see. It's well into Saturday morning, **Ted, Danny** *and* **Charlotte** *are sitting on an old sofa outside. The door to the party is to the back of the stage, the sofa is in a little yard that leads out to the street. Maybe some grass, or just concrete. They're wasted, eyes rolling, jaws tight, sipping water, swallowing, skin dirty, looking monstrous, feeling glamorous. They should all have their little MDMA tics,[19] either crooked fingers pointing their words out, or something in their faces. Post pill gremlins.* **Charlotte** *is physically with them (they're all touching each other somehow, at all times) but her mind seems elsewhere.*

Ted   Anthony. Did you ever call him Anthony?

Danny   No, only his Mum called him that.

Charlotte   I called him Ant sometimes.

Ted   Anthony. Sounds like a different guy, don't it?

Danny   Does your Mum call you Edward?

Ted   No. Does yours?

Danny   No, I meant, like, Ted short for Edward.

Ted   Nah, just plain old Ted, mate.

Danny   My mum calls me Daniel.

Ted   Suits you.

Danny   Good. Suits you too.

Ted   What does?

Danny   That big fuckin' face of yours.

Ted   What about it?

Danny   Suits you. Just lovely.

Ted   Thanks, Dan. I try my best you know, I do try.

Danny   I look at your face, and I think, you know, I known it so long. I know every fuckin' bit of your face. It looks just like your face. Know what I mean? Fuckin' hell, I can't believe it. How long we been mates?

Ted   Yeah. Weird, eh? Considering how much we hate each other.

Danny   You have to ruin it don't you?

Ted   I'm just joking, you know I'm joking. I think we're lucky really. I do, and we are, ain't we, us three?

Danny   Yeah.

Ted   Some people don't have mates.

Danny   No.

Ted   It's been really getting me down recently, you know.

Danny   What has, mate?

Ted   Oh, you know, work, and the routine, and Sally and me, the flat, and who's doing the washing up, and who's making the dinner or, you know. It's. I dunno. I ain't really been seeing a lot of anyone else. Lost contact with a lot of people, I suppose. It's life though, innit. Getting older. But, sometimes Dan, I link up with you, and I think, what a cunt, you know? Coz, you don't have any of those kind of worries do you? The fuckin' rush hour on the Tube, and the telly and the pub quiz. You just naff around being interesting, and I think, what a prick. You know. But, it's life, innit. Coz, obviously, you're not a prick. But, you know. It's good to get out, innit? Come out and party. I didn't want to. I'm kind of done with all this. Done with it all. You know? After what happened. But, I've had a fuckin' great night, ain't I?

Danny   Well, that's nice, mate.

Ted   Obviously I don't mean I actually think you're a prick, Dan.

Danny   No. Course not.

Ted   You know what I mean though, don't ya?

Danny   Mate. I'm a fuckin' mess. Right state. You? You got it sorted. Got a lovely girlfriend, steady job, nice flat. You got it sorted.

Ted   It's boring though. That's what I'm saying. You? You party hard. Me? I hardly party. Everything's exciting for you. Behind the bar or on the dole, or doing some shifts here and there. Every day something different for you. No responsibilities. You're off on tour. Alright, maybe only a tour of Croydon,[20] but still. Off you go.

Charlotte   Oh shut up, the pair of you are doing great. Trust me. You boys are fine. I'm the one should be complaining. I woke up one morning and I was basically my Nan.

Danny   What? Nah. You got a steady job, good prospects, you're doing something you love.

Ted

Charlotte   I spend my life trying to keep fourteen-year-olds from sending each other pictures of their cocks.

Danny   'Svery important. If anyone's alright out of the three of us, it's you, Charlotte.

Ted   We have had some good times though, ain't we? All us lot. I mean, I don't remember exactly what happened or anything. But we did though, didn't we?

Danny   Yeah. We had a right laugh.

Ted   And it's good, innit? Have a night out, feels better than I remember. God, I feel, I feel great. It's lovely. It feels lovely.

Danny   Well, you deserve it, mate. You work hard, don't ya?

Ted   Yeah. I do, you know. I do.

Danny   Well, have a night out then.

Ted   And it's not like I ain't got plans.

Charlotte   What are your plans, Ted?

Ted   Well, you know, I got lots of plans. Shit, actually, you know, well, loads. I make plans all the time. I mean, we could have a plan together, couldn't we?

Danny   Like what?

Ted   Well, I been thinking about a business. My own business, get a start up loan or one a them …

Charlotte   What kind of business?

Ted   Oh, something. You know. What do we need? Now? What do we need that we can't get?

Danny   Delivery booze.[21]

Ted   Ah! Genius! Perfect that. Fuckin' right on the fuckin' nose, bang on the money, perfect. Absolutely fuckin' yes, mate. Twenty-four hour delivery booze, cold beers, curly straws in your cocktail, little sparklers. That's it. We're in business.

Danny   Let's do it then, shall we?

Ted   Yeah, we'll get one a them vans, like a burger van, but it'll be a bar, dead swish. We'll wear dickie bows. And we'll pull up outside whatever house ordered the booze, and bish bash bosh. There you go.

Danny   Mate, we could make a mint.

Ted   We could call it Bar Bros.

Danny   Who's Barbara?

Ted   No, like Bar Brothers.

Danny   That's a shit name.

Ted   I know, but all names are shit when you come up with them; takes a while, don't it, to sink in.

Danny   We should call it wine wine wine, like 999.

Ted   That's fuckin' shit.

Danny   Better than bar bros.

Charlotte   We should call it Drink Drivers.

Danny   That's wicked! What about Pissed Stop. Like pit stop.

Ted   Definitely not calling it pissed stop.

Charlotte   Wait. Wait … I got it … We should call it – Van Rouge. Like, Vin Rouge.[22]

Ted   Well, whatever, point is, I wanna do so much. That's what it is. There's so much I wanna do, and when it hits you. Like, I swear, the other day, we had it all to come, didn't we? And now, I hardly see you, but I love you. Pair of you. I love you both. So much. And, I want you to be happy. You know. Both of you. Together.

Charlotte   We love you too, Ted. You're lovely.

Danny   Oh … Van Rouge!

Ted   Mate, see what was we saying earlier? Well, now's your chance, right? One chance you said, well, here it is. Seize the moment, mate. It's a beautiful morning. First day of the rest of your life and all that. And like, all life is, is moments, right? Tiny little moments, and if you don't make the most of the moment, then you ain't making the most of your life. Right?

He scrambles to his feet, falls off the sofa, manages to keep the whisky at the right angle so as not to spill any.

Just stretching me legs. I be back soon. Right? Good. Right then. See you in a bit. Lovely.

He staggers offstage. They sit there in silence for a moment.

Charlotte   That was weird.

Danny   Teddy, innit.

Charlotte

Danny   It's a good party.

Charlotte   Yeah, it's alright.

Danny   You feel good?

Charlotte   Yeah. I'm fucked, Dan.

Danny   Me too. Want some of this? (*Cigarette.*)

Charlotte   Yeah, go on then.

Danny   Amazing, innit.

Charlotte   Pretty good, yeah.

Danny   Think it's the best fag I ever smoked.

Charlotte   It's definitely a contender.

Danny   I feel great. Do you feel great?

Charlotte   Ted's having fun, ain't he?

Danny   Yeah, innit.

Charlotte   It's good. It's good to see.

Danny   You hear him on the mic earlier?

Charlotte   Don't lie! Ted was on the mic?

Danny   Yeah. For ages as well.

Charlotte   Bless him.

Danny   He was pretty good as it goes.

Charlotte   What was it he used to call himself?

Danny   Tough Ted.

Charlotte   Oh yeah, Tough Ted and Tone Deaf! I'd forgotten about that.

Danny   Remember when it happened?

Charlotte   What?

Danny   Tony.

Charlotte   What about it?

Danny   Ted was there, wasn't he.

Charlotte   Does he ever talk about it?

Danny   Not to me.

Charlotte   Fuckin' hell.

Danny   I think it just got him in a different way.

Charlotte   Poor guy.

Danny   He ain't really come out since.

Charlotte   I don't blame him.

Danny   But he's having it now, ain't he?

Charlotte   It's nice here. Nice just sitting here, innit.

Danny   Look, Charlotte, last night was great.

Charlotte   Yeah, it was.

Danny   I been thinking about it all day.

Charlotte   Yeah, me too.

Danny   There's so much I wanna say to you.

Charlotte   Me too.

Danny   But I don't know how.

Charlotte   Yeah. I know.

Danny   Coz I have, you know, I've really changed.

Charlotte   Yeah, so have I.

Danny   And it's all gonna be different from now on.

Charlotte   Yeah. It is.

Danny   Coz I've seen the light, Charlotte. I get it now. I was a knob, but now I'm alright. I'm a fuckin' –. I'm a changed man. I mean it.

Charlotte   I know you mean it.

Danny   So, what I'm saying is, you've got nothing to be scared of. You can just let yourself go. And it'll all be OK. And you don't have to be angry with me anymore.

Charlotte   Yeah, I know.

Danny   Coz I love you, Charlotte.

Charlotte   I'm leaving Dan. I'm going away.

Danny   What?

Charlotte   I booked a flight. That's it.

Danny   What? What d'you mean you're going away?

Charlotte   I'm gonna travel. Live abroad. Teach.

Danny   How long for?

Charlotte   Year or two.

Danny   What? When?

Charlotte   In like five hours or something.

Danny   What? You joking?

Charlotte   No. No, I'm not joking.

Danny   Why?

Charlotte   Why? Coz I've been in the same part of town my whole life. I could live anywhere in the world, anywhere, but I've never even moved across the river. I want an adventure. I could go to teach somewhere completely new. I could be helping people.

Danny   You can't go.

Charlotte   Why not?

Danny   Well, you teach here. What about your job?

Charlotte   It's all sorted.

Danny   What about your flat?

Charlotte   My sister's gonna take the room.

Danny   Well, what about me then?

Charlotte   I can't waste anymore of my time waiting for someone else to make me happy.

Danny   You don't have to wait.

Charlotte   I need to do this, Dan.

Danny   Well, *I'll* wait for *you* then. I'll wait for you, Charlotte, coz I love you and I wanna be –

Charlotte   You won't wait.

Danny   I fuckin' will! I will.

Charlotte   You won't, Dan. You say it because it seems like the thing to say. You want it to be a big romantic gesture. But it isn't, I know you too well. You might miss me, after you've got home with some girl you met at a party and she's said something stupid, but you won't wait. Coz the thing is, Dan, you can't put anyone else's feelings in front of your own. It's not that you don't want to, it's that you don't know how.

Danny   I do know how. Take as long as you need. I'll be here. And when you come back I'll prove it. I don't want no one else. There's no one else for me. I'll wait for you.

Charlotte   I don't want to hear you saying things that sound nice coz you think I want to hear them. I want you to be honest.

Danny   I am being honest.

Charlotte   It's OK to say – I'm gutted, and I'll miss you. That's enough. You don't have to tell me that you're gonna be heartbroken and fuckin' celibate, coz it's just not true. I know what you're like. I gave you so many chances. And every time you showed me that you didn't really care. Not really. Not when it came down to it.

Danny   Don't go, Charlotte. I don't want you to go.

Charlotte   Come with me then.

Danny   What?

Charlotte   Go pack a bag, get your passport. I'll meet you at the airport. Let's do it if you want to, Dan. Let's go. Me and you.

Danny   What, now?

Charlotte   Yeah.

Danny   Well, obviously I can't just, I mean, you know, it's –. The band. We're a unit. I can't just leave. And work, I mean my name's on the rota till next month. And I gotta feed Dillinja while mum's at my auntie's. I can't just go like that. I can't.

Charlotte *stands up, starts getting her things together. They stand looking at each other, he goes to kiss her, she moves away, kisses his face and walks offstage. He stands there looking like he's been kicked in the guts. She doesn't look back. He stares after her until she's gone.*

Ted   Where's Charlotte?

Danny   Gone.

Ted   What do you mean, gone?

Danny   I mean gone, mate.

Ted   What, gone home, or –?

Danny   Nah, like gone, gone away.

Ted   Gone away?

Danny   She's booked a flight. She's off, mate. Travelling. She's gone. She just. Left.

Ted   Fuck.

Danny   I know.

Ted   You alright?

Danny   Yeah.

Ted   Ah, mate.

Danny   It's alright. It's not a thing.

Ted   You ask her to stay?

Danny   No.

Ted   You gonna go after her?

Danny   What? Nah. Nah. I couldn't.

Ted   Why not?

Danny   What, like, go with her?

Ted   Yeah. Why not?

Danny   Well, you know, we got this gig next week. You know, a big one. Might be some labels there.

Ted   You're joking, right?

Danny   No.

Ted   Mate. I ain't being funny, right? But I known you a long time, and every week of your life you got a gig, and it's always gonna be a big one, and there's always gonna be some label there, but there never is, is there? It's just some dirty little bar that people think is cool coz the drinks are expensive and no one's fuckin' smiling. Every week, mate. And you ain't been signed yet.

Danny   So?

Ted   So? Danny. I'm sorry, but your band's no good, mate. I'm sorry. But, mate – your band's fuckin' shit.

Danny   What?

Ted   I'm sorry, mate.

Danny   Prick.

Ted   True though, innit?

Danny   Fuck off.

Ted   Mate, just this morning you're chewing my ear off about this girl. I'm just sat there, trying to have a peaceful beer, give a little time to remembering our mate, and there you are, Charlotte this, Charlotte that; I've changed Ted, I've changed. I want more. I've had an epiphany.

Danny   So?

Ted   So what?

Danny   So, what you saying?

Ted   I'm saying, that I told you, Dan, I told you you had to take your chance.

Danny   Did you know she was leaving?

Ted   You know what your problem is, mate? You just sit around, expecting life to happen for you. Waiting for it all to just land in

your fuckin' lap. You've never failed, Dan. You've never fuckin'
failed. You've never tried. You need to fuckin' try at least once,
Dan, really fuckin' go for it and try.

Danny   What you talking about?

Ted   I'm talking about sacrifice, Dan. What life's all about. You
gotta grow up, mate. Put yourself second. You know, you don't
have a right to happiness, Dan. You can't just, you know, get it. It's
hard, innit, life. It's tough. And loving someone, that's hard too.
It's not meant to be roses and blow jobs forever. It's fuckin' hard
work. It's commitment, mate. It's knowing the kind of day she's
had just by hearing the way her key turns in the door.

Danny   Alright, Ted. Jesus. Alright.

Ted   What? I'm serious. you just need to make a decision, and
fuckin' stick to it.

Danny   A decision?

Ted   That's all it is, Dan. You decide. You say to yourself, I love
this girl. I fuckin' love this girl, and then, if a couple years go
by and it don't feel the same no more, well fuck it, because you
remember your decision. That's what I'm saying about happiness.
It's not getting exactly what you want whenever you fuckin' want
it with the least possible effort – it's about being alright with what
you have. Just that. That's all it is.

Danny *smokes a cigarette,* **Ted** *leans his head back against the
wall.*

Ted   You should go after her, mate.

Danny   I can't.

Ted *rushes.*

Ted   Why not?

Danny   Are you happy, Ted?

Ted   Rushing my fuckin' tits off, ain't I? I'm well happy.

Danny   You know what I mean, Ted. I don't mean now, I mean
like, in general.

Ted   Oh, *in general*? No, course not. No one is. No one we know anyway. Look at us all, eating these little funny buttons just so we can smile at each other without looking away.

Danny   You are looking away.

Ted   Am I? Oh.

Danny   Coz I ain't happy, mate. I ain't. I mean, I'm alright, I don't mean to get all fuckin' emo about it but –

Ted   I tell you what it is, right? It's the little things that make me happy. Stupid things. Like, you know, for example – I hate my job, right? I hate it. I wake up in the morning and I feel sick about my life. But I like it when I see two cars the same colour parked next to each other. I like smoking cigarettes on cold days. I like it when someone makes me a cup of tea, just how I like it, without me having to ask. I like it when Sally laughs with her mouth full. I like quiz shows. I like it that elephants bury their dead. I'll never be anybody's fuckin' hero, right? I'll never be celebrated, and I'll never look at myself in the mirror and say that's right hot shot, you're the fuckin' man. But I like listening to the radio. And fuck it, I like it when Sally's brother invites me round to watch the rugby, even though I hate the fuckin' rugby, coz it shows he's trying. Know what I mean? Do you, Dan? Do you know what I mean?

They sit there, **Danny** *thinks about what* **Ted** *has said.* **Ted** *seems a bit spent after the outburst. They smoke a cigarette.*

Danny   Come on then, Ted; you buying me breakfast or what?

Chorus Three

One   Everything was

Two   Brighter,

One   There was no more exhaustion.

Three   The moments were all glorious, and full of importance.

Two   But now your jaw's clenched,

Three   You feel sick

Two   And a bit like you're

One   Falling,

Three   As your

One   Night

Two   Steps

Three   On the toes of their

One   Morning –

Three   These

One   Other

Two   People

One   On the street

Three   Walking,

Two   People who've slept and got up.

One   The rain's

Two   Pouring,

Three   You feel the guilt chasing you down,

One   Your soul's

Three   Roaring

Two   That there must be a way to be more than this.

Three   Life in a city of awkwardness –

One   We should have been monoliths,

Three   Could have had everything,

Two   We know we've got more to give.

One   Our skin holds our bones in, our organs are moaning,

Three   Coz it feels like

Two   Nothing means nothing,

Three   But we need to feel

All   Something.

One   Three friends, knee deep in the weekend,

Two   In their own ways, they're all steeped in pretence

One   And what they want's

Three   More,

Two   Something real they can

Three   Touch –

One   Well – you only know what's enough,

Three   When you know what's more than enough.

Scene Four

Greasy spoon café. **Ted** *reads the tabloids. Cups of tea or coffee in front of them. No food.*

Ted   You hear what that woman said when we got off the bus?

Danny   What woman?

Ted   She had her kid with her, and we walked past and the kid looked at me, and the woman put her hand over his eyes and said 'don't look at the man'.

Danny   Fuck.

Ted   We must look a right fright.

Danny   You look lovely, babe.

Ted   Prick.

Danny   You think you could eat?

Ted   Worth a try, ain't it?

Danny   Yeah. S'pose.

Ted   I feel horrible.

Danny   Me too.

Ted   Was a good night, though, wa'n'it?

Danny   Yeah, mate. Great night.

Ted   I do feel horrible though.

Pause. They drink their tea. **Ted** *looks at menu.* **Danny** *picks up the paper, looks through it.*

Ted   What's happening in the real world, then?

Danny (*flicking through the pages*)   Oh, you know, war, dead civilians, fear-mongering about religious fundamentalism, footballer that cheated on his wife, someone's tits, couple criminally insane school children. Parrot found in Putney[23] that can rap the first verse of the Fresh Prince of Bel Air[24] theme tune.

Ted   Usual then.

Danny   I hate reading the paper. Don't matter where you go in the world, does it, everywhere's fucked. Everything's fucked.

Ted   Pie 'n' mash?[25] That be too much, you reckon?

Danny   Makes you think though, dunnit? We might think we got it bad here, like, think we're struggling, but we're fine. Look at us. We're fine. Compared to some of the shit going on. This is luxury, mate; you know what I mean?

Ted   Probably is too much, innit?

Danny   There's always someone worse off than you though, ain't there?

Ted   Depends how big the portions are I s'pose.

Danny   It's always safer to look around and say, no matter how fucked I am, it could be worse.

Ted   Look, that guy's got a jacket potato. Maybe that's what I need. Beans though? Couldn't manage beans.

Danny   And that's it, innit? That's the whole point? As long as you think that, why would you risk it?

Ted   If in doubt, head for the classic.

Danny   Changing things, I mean. Making things better.

Ted   Full English.[26]

Danny (*still looking through the paper*)   I mean, this can't be what it's all been for … *This* …

Ted   That's it, mate. That's the one. Stick to what you know, eh? Don't break it if it ain't fixed. Full English, no beans, extra hash brown. Bosh. You ready to order yet or what?

Danny   I could go meet her, couldn't I? At the airport. Just sit and have a coffee with her or something? I don't have to get on the plane. Just go be there. Show her. That's showing her, ain't it?

Ted   What you having?

Danny   I'll have what you're having.

Ted   Nope. No, you don't. I ain't having you throwing a strop coz I didn't get you no bubble and squeak.[27]

Danny   I just can't seem to get it right with her.

Ted   You're more fussy than you think, you know.

Danny   No, I'm not.

Ted   Tomatoes?

Danny   Fuckin' hate tomatoes.

Ted   See?

Danny   Everything I do, I always end up the cunt.

Ted   White or brown?

Danny   What?

Ted   Bread.

Danny   I feel horrible.

Ted (*phone ringing*)   Sorry, mate. It's Sal. I gotta, hold on … (*In a coupley, sickly sweet voice we haven't heard from him until now.*) Hello darlin'. You alright? Oh, lovely. Great. Yeah. Yeah I'm fine thanks, babe. Just in the caff[28] now, yeah, it was nice yeah, we went for a couple of pints, then watched a film, nothing special … Just me and Dan … What, now? IKEA?[29] Well, I was gonna just have a bit of brekkie, and then just go back to Dan's for a … yeah? Yeah, I know I seen him all night, but you know. It's been a while since … Oh yep, no, I know, the curtains. I know. Course. I'm sorry … yep. No, OK. Well, I'll walk up now then … yep, OK, on the corner. No, I won't be. Alright then, babe. Yep, love you too. Yep. Alright. Bye, darling. Bye …

Sorry, mate, I gotta go. Sorry. It's 'er, you know. Duty calls.

Danny   Yeah, yeah. All good.

Ted   You'll be alright, wont ya?

Danny   Fine mate, don't be silly.

Ted   You gonna, you be about later? Maybe see you in the pub?

Danny   Yeah, give us a shout.

Ted   Alright, mate. I had a great night, Dan. We should do it more often, feels like it's been ages. You know what I mean?

Danny   Yeah, too long.

Ted   I meant it, earlier.

Danny   What?

Ted   You're my best mate, Dan.

Danny   Ain't so bad yourself, mate.

Ted   Look, I'm gonna go follow my girlfriend round IKEA for the next four fuckin' hours, I feel like I just swallowed a planetarium or something. I'm fuckin' munted, and I'm gonna go and hold Sally's hand and look at curtains and toothbrush holders and lampshades and it's gonna be fuckin' tragic. But I'm gonna do it. Coz that's what she needs me to do. Know what I mean?

Danny   Planetarium?

Ted   Dan, what the fuck are you doing here?

Danny   What?

Ted   Sat here in the same old fuckin' caff again.

Danny   Up until a minute ago, mate, it was good enough for you.

Ted   Go and find her, Dan. If that's what you want. Make the decision, and go for it.

Danny   I don't know, Ted. I don't know. I'm alright, don't worry about me. I know what I'm doing. You want another pill[30] 'fore you get to IKEA?

Ted   What? Nah, I'm done mate. I'm fuckin' done.

Danny   Suit yourself.

Ted   Later on then, Dan.

Danny   Later on, Ted.

Sits there for a moment, staring ahead, sounds of the café get really loud. Grease frying and the radio and people talking. He drops a pill. Winces.

Danny   You're lucky really.

If you'd have lived 'til now you would have just got fat and boring like the rest of us. You wouldn't have been no different.

You never got old enough to see your mate become the weirdo with a drugs lisp, looking like he's just found fishbones in his mouth, nodding to himself. In a Slammin Vinyl[31] bomber jacket.

It used to feel like we was doing something that no one else had ever done. But really we was just getting fucked. And all them other kids that weren't cool enough to hang about with us, them ones we sold screwed up bits of clingfilm to for a tenner a go, they all grew up nicely, didn't they? They went off to uni and reinvented themselves and now they're doctors, replacing people's limbs in war zones, or they're professional cricketers, or they're working in the fuckin' city, blowing a ton on coke every night and fuckin' women that wouldn't even look at me if I was hanging in a gallery.

So you're lucky. Coz if you was still here, you'd have a habit, or depression, or anxiety attacks, or all three, and you'd be making secret plans to run away and start again in a new fuckin' country where no one knows how much of a fuckin' wreck you are, or, you'd be up to your neck in debt, fuckin' a bird that thinks you're a dick and checking your Twitter[32] every twenty-two seconds to see if anyone's said anything about your fuckin' shit band. We used to be the fuckin' boys, mate. Now, the highlight of my day is taking a good shit.

I miss her already. I never meant to take her for granted, Tony. But you do, don't you. It's like air. You never know how much it means to you till you're drowning. And then it's too late.

If I could turn around and be the Danny that I want to be, the Danny that lives in my head, then shit, she'd never stop smiling. But the thing is, mate, I ain't that guy, I'm this guy. Alone in the caff with the horrors coming on, still ain't come up off the last pill I done, wishing I could be braver and just sweep her off her feet. But she's gone, ain't she. She's had enough, off she fuckin' trots. She's the only person that ever made me happy, Tony, the only person that ever really knew me, and she thinks I'm a cunt.

And alright I probably am. But who fuckin' isn't? You were a cunt. Who really, deep down inside, isn't a complete cunt? At least I'm ready to try.

I want to be on stage in front of thousands of screaming fans, doing something fuckin' great, and smiling like it's no big deal. But every time I sit down to practice my guitar, I end up fantasising about sell-out shows while I play the same shitty riff I been playing for years. And you know what, it's kind of the same with her.

And as it is I got nothing going on. Not really. Ted thinks I got this glamourous lifestyle, but it's all bullshit, I hang out with people that spend the whole night looking over my shoulder in case something more interesting's happening behind me, and they all think my band's a joke, I mean, they think we're actually joking, but we're not. And all my songs are fuckin' shit. Well, 'she purrs my motorbike' is actually pretty good but fuck sake, I work in a bar and I have an epiphany every other fuckin' day, then as soon as I got a couple beers in me I'm back to square one, repeating the same conversations I've had a thousand times over and creeping around looking for someone to give me a line and I don't want to be this man anymore.

Thing is, in a few hours – I'll be staring at her name on my phone, too late to call, coz she'll be gone, and I'll just be sat there like a prick, staring at the shape of the letters, the way they fit together, so perfect, just like her, and I'll sit there, wishing I could show her that when I'm with her I feel so fuckin' real, like, not pretending nothing, just who I am. I feel like I can be the man I want to be. And I do want to be that man, Tony. I do. But for some reason. For some fuckin' reason.

And then I'll catch my reflection in between the letters of her name, face like a car crash, and I'll make the same fuckin' promises I make every morning. Tell myself I'm changing things. That this is it.

But then I suppose, if we could all be the men we wanted to be, this caff would be full of secret agents and movie stars, wouldn't it? As it is, Tony, it's that guy drinking milk and talking to the walls, that guy eating beans with no teeth, and me. All of us, regretting the decisions we never had the guts to make.

And she's gone. She's fuckin' gone.

So you're lucky really.

Chorus Four

Two   And so,

One   We have music,

Two   We have love,

One   We have each other,

Three   But it ain't enough.

Two   So we get ruined, taking drugs to feel,

One   And it feels

All   Good.

Two   Coz in these vacant sub-day days that turn the blood,

One   You touch my face,

Three   You wake me up.

One   We love this city, it raised us up,

Two   Told us to brace ourselves against the flood.

Three   It taught us all we

Two   Know,

One   And this is all we came to

Two   Show –

Three   That times are strange,

Two   As all times are,

Three   Our minds are strained,

Two   Our eyes

Three   Wine dark,

One   Our lives are played like dice or cards,

Three   But our hearts are good, and wear their scars.

Two   We look up, but there's no

One   Stars,

Two   Just streetlights burning down on broken cars

One   And in us, churning guts,

Three   Unspoken

Two   Trust,

One   Closed eyes with our minds

Two   Opened up –

One   The old mantra learned that soaks us up –

Three   It's best if you don't hope for much.

Scene Five

Charlotte *is sitting in the park, looking at Tony's tree.* **Danny** *walks up, sees her. She's swigging from a bottle of whisky, he's carrying a can of K cider.*[33] *It's late afternoon.*

Danny   Charlotte?

Charlotte   Alright, Dan.

Danny   What you doing here? I thought you was

Charlotte   I come to say goodbye.

Danny   What time's the flight?

Charlotte   I missed it.

Danny   What?

Charlotte   It leaves in an hour.

Danny   So, you ain't going?

Charlotte   No. I ain't.

Danny   That's great Charlotte. How come?

Starts rolling a joint.

Charlotte   Loads of reasons. Mainly coz I'm fucked, and the idea of customs was making me wanna be sick. Honestly, I feel like my face is doing interpretive dance.

Danny   It's ballet.

Charlotte   What, The Nutcrackhead?

Danny   No, ballet.

Lighting the joint.

Charlotte   I ain't been here all year, you know?

Danny   No?

Charlotte   No.

Danny   He wouldn't mind.

Charlotte   And I was thinking, the best thing I can do to celebrate his memory, is make something of my life. Know what I mean, Dan?

Danny   Yeah, for real. Definitely.

Charlotte   I'm gonna go back to school and teach. Properly. Coz I love them kids. And they deserve so much more. They really do. Last thing they need is another person walking out on them. I'm gonna put all my energy into it, Dan. I'm gonna be a teacher. A really fuckin' good one.

Danny   Yeah, you should do that, Charlotte.

Taking out some coke and doing a bump[34] *off the corner of a card. He offers one to* **Charlotte**. *She goes for it.*

Charlotte   Or something. I don't know. Something.

Danny   Yeah. I think you're right. And like, I know what you mean, coz, I been thinking too, I'm gonna do it you know? With the band, and all that, I'm gonna fuckin' do it. It's gonna be huge.

Charlotte   Yeah?

Danny   Yeah. Hard work, innit. Just gotta keep working at it.

Charlotte   That's right, yeah.

Danny   Practice innit, six hours a day. Straight. And I'm thinking about a martial art too. For the discipline.

Charlotte   Oh yeah?

Danny   Yeah, the breathing and that, the posture. I think I might start training.

Charlotte   Yeah, you should. That'd be good for you.

Danny   Yeah. Or yoga or something.

Charlotte   Yeah?

Danny   Yeah. Might start going classes.

Charlotte   Yoga, yeah?

*He passes the joint. Swigs from his can. Lines up another bump.
And one for her.*

Danny   And I'm gonna cut down on the sniff[35] and that. Cut
down on all of it. Stop wasting my time. Know what I mean? Get
my shit together.

Charlotte   Yeah. Me too.

Danny   And you reckon, if you're sticking around, could I, like,
another time maybe, take you out? Like, we could take things
slow, couldn't we? If you're staying, there's no hurry is there. Next
week, the week after?

Charlotte   I don't think so, Dan.

Danny   Coz, you know, I'm changing things. I am. I'll show you,
Charlotte, I'm sorting myself out.

Charlotte   Yeah, I am too, Dan. I am.

Danny   Does make you think though don't it, day like today.

Charlotte   Yeah. It does.

Danny   I do mean it, I am, I'm sorting myself out.

Charlotte   Me too, Dan. Definitely.

Danny (*surprised*)   Fuck.

Charlotte   What?

Danny   I feel fucked, you know.

Charlotte (*happy*)   Me too, fuckin' wasted.

They have another bump each. Swig some whisky. **Danny** *puts his
arm around her.*

Chorus Five

One   How many times you dreamed of

Two *and* **Three**   Something,

Three   Then told yourself your dreams ain't

One *and* **Two**   Nothing?

Two   The thing is though, your dreams are

One *and* **Three**   More

One   Than just something that came before you shook them off,

Three   Your dreams are worth pursuing,

Two   Mate,

Three   You do deserve everything you dare to want,

One   But you'll never

One *and* **Two**   Fly

Two   'Til you're prepared to

Two *and* **Three**   Jump.

One   So here's the thing then –

Three   Here's the closing –

One   Once,

Two   That breaking wave was just a frozen raindrop

Three   Waiting for its cloud to open and let it fall,

One   So let it call your name –

Two   That thing inside you screaming,

Three   There is

All   More

Two   To you than your routine.

One   We came here to share the feeling

Three   That until you live the things you're dreaming

Two   They'll stay

One   Private, behind

Two   Eyelids –

Three   That's the point – we came to speak it –

One   All the things you hope in secret you could be –

All   You are –

Two   We mean it.

Three   Whatever moves you – you must chase it –

One   Stand before it – mate – embrace it

Two   Life wants you – it beckons – makes itself immense –

Three   Respect it – take it in your arms,

One   Connect and face it.

Three   Your life is for

All   Much more

One   Than getting

All   Wasted.

We see projections of supermarket aisles, pubs, people in a party, then riots, revolts, soldiers, burning cars etc., interspersed with the three characters, buying cigarettes, lying on the floor of their flat, watching telly, time-lapse footage of London, pizza boxes, traffic jams, market stalls, queue in the bank, then **Ted***, in IKEA, pushing a trolley loaded up with loads of massive flat pack boxes, struggling, Egypt after the revolution, Tony's tree, kids in a classroom, visuals flicker off, like when you turn a telly off with a remote, goes to a flat line, then a dot, then flicker back on and there's a camera inside an IKEA box,* **Ted** *opens it, starts pulling out planks of wood, it flickers, the box closes, back to blackness.*

Music still playing, the characters are back on stage in their first positions, it's Monday again, nothing changes, **Ted***'s still at work,* **Charlotte** *is still in the classroom,* **Danny** *is still up sniffing lines with his mates. They look tired. Lonely.*

End.

Notes

1   Magic FM: an independent radio station based in London that plays popular music. This station is also referenced on the track 'The Truth' on Tempest's album *Everybody Down*.

2   Babycham: a sparkling alcoholic drink, popular in the 1960s and 1970s.

3   jacked: a colloquial term meaning 'stole' or 'thieved'.

4   spliffs: marijuana cigarettes.

5   rock pipes: glass pipes used to smoke rocks of crack cocaine.

6   skunk: a potent type of marijuana.

7   pissed: colloquial term meaning inebriated by alcohol.

8   custard creams: a popular sandwich biscuit, with a firm cream centre.

9   skinning up: colloquial term meaning to roll a marijuana cigarette.

10   MDMA: 3,4-Methylenedioxymethamphetamine, a powder form of the recreational drug ecstasy.

11   joint: another colloquial term for a marijuana cigarette.

12   Peckham: an area of south-east London. Known in the late twentieth century as an ethnically diverse working-class district, it became increasingly fashionable in the 2010s and beyond as a result of gentrification and the wider urban development of London.

13   Ketamine: a hallucinogenic recreational drug.

14   killing each other over postcodes: refers to gang violence happening between young people from different districts of London. A postcode is a set of letters and numbers used to signify particular districts for the purposes of mail delivery.

15   Tescos: a popular supermarket chain.

16   Rizla: a popular brand of cigarette rolling paper.

17   munted: colloquial phrase meaning inebriated on drugs and/or alcohol.

18   bass heavy: colloquial phrase meaning that one can feel the throb on the bass of the music.

19   MDMA tics: the physical signs that you've consumed MDMA.

20   Croydon: a large town in south London, not glamorous; a flashpoint for the 2011 riots discussed in the CONTEXT section of the introduction.

21   booze: colloquial term for alcohol.

22   vin rouge: French for 'red wine'.

23   Putney: a district in south-west London.

24   Fresh Prince of Bel Air: a popular 1990s sitcom, fronted by the actor Will Smith, with a novelty hip hop theme tune.

25 pie 'n' mash: a traditional London dish of meat pie and mashed potatoes.

26 Full English: a traditional cooked breakfast usually including bacon, sausage, egg, beans and toast, with other optional elements such as tomato, black pudding, hash browns etc.

27 bubble and squeak: traditional British breakfast dish of fried leftover vegetables, usually including cabbage and potatoes.

28 caff: colloquial local pronunciation of 'café'.

29 IKEA: a popular furniture store.

30 pill: slang for a recreational drug in tablet form, usually ecstasy.

31 Slammin Vinyl: a brand specializing in rave and hardcore music; runs a record label and events and sells merchandise.

32 Twitter: a social media platform where users communicate using short messages called 'tweets'.

33 K cider: a cheap brand of cider with a very high alcohol content.

34 doing a bump: snorting a small amount of cocaine to ease the feeling of withdrawal.

35 sniff: colloquial term for cocaine.